INVITATION TO VISION

IDEAS AND IMAGINATIONS FOR ART

BROWN

ART SERIES

Edited by

WILLARD F. WANKELMAN
Bowling Green State University
Bowling Green, Ohio

INVITATION TO VISION

IDEAS AND IMAGINATIONS FOR ART

Earl W. Linderman
Chairman, Department of Art • *Arizona State University* • *Tempe, Arizona*

Wm. C. Brown Company Publishers • Dubuque, Iowa

Manufactured by WM. C. BROWN CO. INC., Dubuque, Iowa
Printed in U. S. A.

to *Marlene*

Acknowledgments

The author is grateful to the following organizations and individuals for permission to quote:

ARTFORUM magazine for the quotation by Robert Mallary.

A. S. Barnes & Company, Inc. for the quotation from *The Challenge of Modern Art* by Allen Leepa.

Bell Telephone Laboratories for sending photographs.

California Institute of Technology for permission to use photographs from the Mount Wilson and Palomar Observatories.

Doubleday and Co. for the quotation from *The Voices of Silence,* by André Malraux.

Dr. Edward S. Ross, Curator, California Academy of Sciences for many excellent photographs that he took and developed.

Eastman Kodak Company for the use of several beautiful photographs.

Edmund Scientific Company, 101 E. Gloucester Pike, Barrington, New Jersey, for photographs of Moire patterns.

Faber and Faber, Ltd., for the quotation by Matisse from the book *Matisse From the Life* by Raymond Escholier.

Frederick Ungar Publishing Co., Inc., New York, for the quotation by Lao Tzu from the book *Tao Teh King*. Interpreted as *Nature and Intelligence* by Archie J. Bahm.

George Braziller, Inc. for the quotation from the *Notebooks of Leonardo Da Vinci*, edited by Edward MacCurdy; from the original MacCurdy volumes published by Reynal and Hitchcock.

Harvard University Press for the quotation by Ben Shahn from his book *The Shape of Content*.

Holt, Rinehart and Winston for the quotation from *Understanding the Arts* by Bernard S. Myers.

International Business Machines Corporation for the many photographs they so generously contributed.

Paul Theobald and Company for the quotation by Moholy-Nagy from his book *Vision in Motion*.

Random House, Inc., for the quotations from the book *Letters of The Great Artists* by Richard Friedenthal.

Reinhold Publishing Corporation for the quotation by Eliel Sarrinen from his book *Search For Form*.

San Juan Unified School District for the photograph of Ed Larson, the artist.

Smithsonian Institution, particularly Dr. Richard S. Boardman and Frederick J. Collier for permission to use photographs obtained through the Division of Meteorites, Department of Mineral Sciences.

The Museum of Modern Art for the quotations from *Picasso: Fifty Years of His Art* by Alfred H. Barr, Jr. and for several photographs.

Thomas Y. Crowell Co. for the quotation from the book *Poems of William Blake* by Amelia H. Mŭnson.

United States Department of Agriculture, Forest Service, Madison, Wisconsin for photographs.

University of California Press for the quotation by Arnheim from his book *Art and Visual Perception*.

University of Minnesota, Department of Art, *40 American Painters, 1940-1950*, 1951, p. 33.

Wesleyan University Press for the quotation by James J. Gibson in his article "Pictures, Perspective, and Perception" from the book *The Visual Arts Today*, edited by Gyorgy Kepes.

The author is particularly grateful to several individuals who aided immeasurably in the creation of this book. They include Ralph Talbert of the Audio-Visual Department of the Sacramento State College who took many of the excellent and difficult photographs which appear in the text; Jon Geil who also spent much time working with the author in specific photographic directions; Boyd Jensen and Nick DeLucia who supplied photographs; Bobbie Climent and Ray Crown, Phil Kennedy; several artists whose work appears throughout the volume, and most of all to Marlene Linderman.

Special acknowledgment should also be noted to David Dangelo, Assistant Director of the Crocker Art Gallery, Sacramento, California, and to Stephen A. Gyermek, Director of the Pioneer Museum and Haggin Galleries, Stockton, California, both of whom supplied photographs.

Preface

This book deals directly with idea sources and possibilities for artistic expression. It is for all students who wish to discover where the raw idea material for art comes from. As such, this is a book of search and inquiry. It offers to the student a series of suggestions that are aimed at stimulating his artistic eye and challenging his awareness.

In the chapters which follow, both man-made and natural forms are explored and discussed in terms of offering idea potential for the production of art products. The first chapter serves as an introduction and underlines the value of becoming perceptually observant of the world about us. The chapter discusses some methods and approaches for establishing a personal attitude that will foster *aesthetic awareness*.

In chapter two, the search for ideas begins with a discussion of the human form in a variety of situations and positions. It seemed best to begin with the figure as it is the dominant image in society. Man has been represented in countless varieties and manners by every culture since the millenniums of aesthetic time began. The figure, whether alone or in a crowd is an integral unit of all situations, and as such is one of the most complicated and challenging of forms. Ideas for interpreting the figure are discussed, including the figure in motion, in darkness, in bright sunlight, sitting, standing, in repose, and many unusual aspects relating to the human form.

Chapters three and four deal with the products that man has created for use. They are viewed in the light of what they can offer to the art student in the way of compositional ideas and other artistic production. For that matter, the entire book has this objective. As such, there is an open-endedness concerning all subject areas which of necessity must remain as beginning approaches. Each art student will extend the ideas contained in this book in his own way.

Chapters five, six, seven, and eight relate to idea discovery in forms of the flora and fauna kingdoms. Emphasis on the detailed structure of various plants, animals, birds, and insects is intended to provide insights not readily apparent in the everyday meeting with such forms. The necessity for tapping one's inquisitive impulses is underscored in each chapter. Discoveries for art come when the art student plunges forth to seek the unusual or to search for new ideas and ways to say what he has experienced.

Chapter nine elucidates the area of precision instruments such as the camera, microscope, magnifying lens, and other optical tools that enable man to capture those aspects of life that would otherwise go undetected before the exploring eye of the artist. Objects which are too minute to be observed, or events which move too rapidly to be noticed with normal vision can be caught by the camera lens. Once the action can be brought within human range it can be focused and expanded in elaborate detail. The artist then has an opportunity to drink deeply of the more fascinating and unusual aspects of the natural and man-made worlds.

Chapters ten and eleven concentrate on the possibilities for discovery in viewing the beauty of sky, land, and water under a multi-tude of conditions. There are literally thousands of possibilities contained in each narrow range of what we observe. As the artist searches, he finds that the initial circle of discovery continues to grow before his discriminating vision. In examining terrain of this nature, the artist can move from the massiveness of space down to the tiniest microscopic particle. Infinity lies at both ends of such an aesthetic viewfinder, and it is all there for the sensitive person to discover and utilize.

The final chapter returns to man and explores ideas and directions found in the works of artists. A close study of paintings and art works in museums, galleries and studios offers suggestions for developing one's own approach to art. Statements by several artists, as well as photographs of their work are included for comparison and discussion. Where fellow artists get their ideas can be quite stimulating.

The value of using pictorial material to suggest ideas has been carefully considered. The photographs are intended to suggest pathways and clues *in their own right,* as well as to enhance the verbal message. In fact, many details concerning specific subject matter could only be adequately presented from the standpoint of the camera. This book does not attempt to be all inclusive in relation to specific directions for art. It is intended to serve as *an invitation to vision.* As such, information is presented that could lead to aesthetic adventures.

Finally, this is a book for all students who would extend the boundaries of their own aesthetic awareness and thus open the doors which can lead to a unique vision.

Earl W. Linderman
Oregon State University

Contents

INVITATION TO VISION

IDEAS AND IMAGINATIONS FOR ART

"We have kept our eyes open to our surroundings, and also our brains . . . . in our subjects, we keep the joy of discovery, the pleasure of the unexpected; our subject itself must be a source of interest. . . ."

"The artist is a receptacle for emotions that come from all over the place: from the sky, from the earth, from a scrap of paper, from a passing shape, from a spider's web. . . .[1]

lph Talbert

Chapter 1

Art Begins
with Idea Awareness

Idea sources for artistic expression can be discovered everywhere! One artist might draw his inspiration from flowers, another from still life arrangements. Another may be moved by the sea. Still another may concentrate on the human figure. The possibilities for art within any given object are virtually without limit. A single piece of fruit, such as an apple, can be interpreted with countless variations.

Ideas for art come from many different types of experiences. Sometimes the beginning threads come from thinking over such experiences as we have had. Letting information jell in our minds often gives it a chance to mature and take root. We can get ideas from

---

[1]From *Picasso: Fifty Years of His Art* by Alfred H. Barr, Jr., copyright 1946 by The Museum of Modern Art, New York, and reprinted with its permission. The first quote, "Statement by Picasso: 1923," was made in Spanish to Marius de Zayas. Picasso approved de Zayas's manuscript before it was translated into English and published, originally, in *The Arts,* New York, May, 1923, under the title, "Picasso Speaks." The second quote is the "Statement of 1935." Christian Zervos put down these remarks of Picasso immediately after a conversation with him at Boisgeloup in 1935. Picasso went over the notes and approved them informally. They were first published under the title "Conversation avec Picasso" in *Cahiers d'Art,* 1935, volume 10, number 10, pp. 173-8. The above translation is based on one by Myfanwy Evans.

investigating specific places and things. First-hand contact with the source of stimulation is probably the most effective means for capturing raw material. Ideas for art could strike at any time. In this respect, it is always a good practice to carry a small notebook in which to put down a quick sketch or other shorthand note. If we let ideas slip through our grasp, they may be gone forever. Recording the first inklings can be a significant step in keeping the thoughts at the surface of our thinking. It also provides us with a record and a basis for future comparisons.

Where do we begin the search for art ideas? During the initial stages, it is important to cultivate a *posture of awareness* so that considerable amounts of information or idea potential will be taken in. This means establishing a perceptual alertness; being able to grasp the details of any experience. The artist must be able to gather a large body of information on any given subject. The more data that he has to work with, the wider his range of possibilities will be when it is time to put his thinking in order. Therefore, in the beginning contacts with a subject, the first ideas should be taken in without immediately focusing on an aesthetic objective. It is better to keep a steady flow of stimuli coming in for mental storage.

In this detailed search to increase one's idea index, we need to establish an intake framework that is equipped to receive the raw source data. Our senses form this network through which the body can bring in signals that will be suitable for manufacture into artistic products. This indicates that we must become observant to the tiny but significant nuances of our experiences. Through examination of the details of an experience, we are better able to build a knowledgeable backlog and have richer possibilities for expression in the art form. Unlike osmosis, the source material for artistic expression does not seep through to us in an aesthetic vacuum. It must be searched out, examined, and then cultivated in our imagination. By increasing our awareness of things we broaden our viewpoints and are ultimately encouraged to seek more daring and original art forms.

Learning to Search for Ideas

The search for idea sources begins when we establish an openness of mind so that information coming in will not be subject to a premature critical judgment. It is essential to let the initial brainstorms filter through until many phases or aspects of an experience can be considered. Refinement of the data comes after all factors are taken into account. To adequately investigate an idea source, one might have to make several trips to the source.

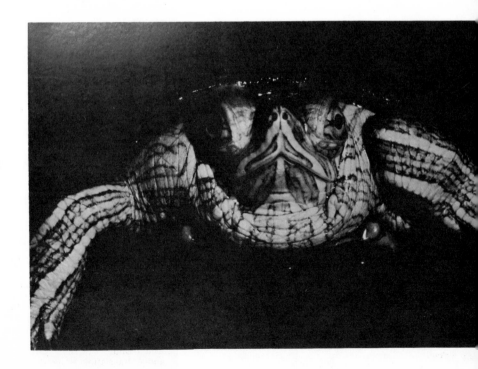

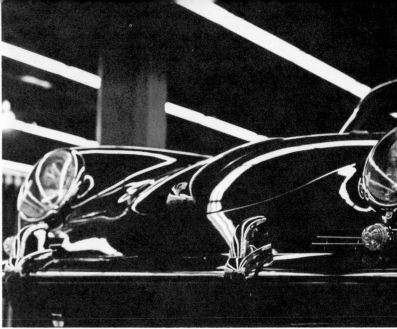

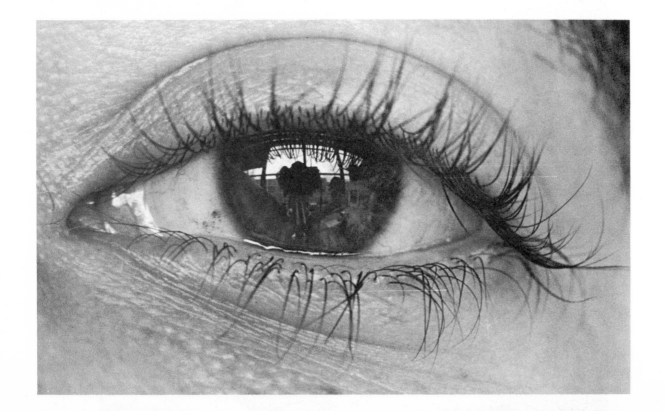

Art ideas can come from everywhere. One must be willing to search and investigate his world in order to discover that which fits his aesthetic eye.

There are unlimited avenues available to the alert person who seeks to gain insight on a subject. If, for example, one decided to investigate "trees," he could begin his search by obtaining a number of books on the subject. This would provide a quantity of technical and biological information, as well as assorted visual examples. Another approach might be to recall past experiences with trees. We all have fleeting images of climbing a tree trunk, swinging on a branch, climbing high on a limb, or just listening to the scrape of a branch against the window. Most of us have seen trees uprooted from storms, or trees that lay dead in a field; or trees that are gnarled from too many storms. We have picked peaches, apples, or plums from a "friendly old fellow" in the orchard. Some experiences will be vague — mere traces of some past memory. The thought of a tree may spark thinking of a more violent nature. We might remember the tree that crashed on a roof top, or a forest that caught fire. Trees might have a special place in our memory, such as the one that caught kites in its branches each spring. Any or all of these experiences with trees could stimulate some beginning ideas for artistic development.

The visual data can be further expanded through firsthand observation, touch, and other sensory means to provide the fullest detailed analysis of trees. In using a direct approach, it is helpful to pose questions. In the case of trees, the following questions may illuminate possible idea material:

Which trees suggest the most interesting character for an art form?
Which trees are massive and rugged in appearance? Which are delicate and stately?
Which trees best express weathering by wind and sea?
How do leaves differ in size, shape, and color from tree to tree?
Are the roots visible on trees?

- Which trees have buds or blossoms? Is there a scent? Does bark have a scent?
Does wood have the same smell when wet?
How do branches move in the breeze?
How does a tree appear when its branches are silhouetted against a sky?
How does a tree appear at night?
How does a tree appear during a rainstorm?
What is the appearance of a tree in the middle of winter?
How does a tree appear against a background of snow?
How does a tree appear with strong sunlight focused on it?
What does a tree look like in a heavy fog?
How do trees appear on a distant mountain slope?
How do trees appear from the air?
How do trees appear when viewed down a mountain slope?
How does a tree appear when viewed straight up?
How does a cluster of trees appear?
How do trees appear that are reflected in water?
What kinds of shadows do trees make?

The artist seeks answers to questions of this nature before making any decision to begin experimentation with art media. Consequently, when he is ready to begin work on the art form, he can draw from a wide repertoire of information. In addition to such thinking, the artist may also collect a portfolio of illustrations, as well as make several "on location" study sketches of specific trees. In this manner, he is able to rely on the sum total of his experiences with trees to aid him in creating a series of original interpretations.

Observing how other artists interpret the problem can be an additional means of gaining insight into the nature of a subject. Observe how Henri Matisse, the great French artist described his thoughts on drawing a tree:

A posture of awareness enables one to perceive relationships as well as differences. What are the similarities in these photographs?

Ralph Talbert

The aesthetic focus can sharpen at either close range or toward the distant terrain. Individual judgment decides what is pertinent to the search.

*As if I had never seen or drawn a tree. I can see one from my
window. I have to take in patiently how the mass of the tree is
made, then the tree itself, the trunk, the branches, the leaves.
First the branches symmetrically placed on one plane. Then,
how the branches twist, passing in front of the trunk. Don't
misunderstand me. I don't mean that, looking at the tree from
my window, I try to copy it. The tree is also a whole series of
effects it has on me. It is not a matter of drawing a tree I see.
I have an object in front of me which produces an effect on my
mind, not only as a tree, but in relation to all sorts of other
feelings. I shan't get rid of my emotion by exactly copying the
tree, in drawing its leaves one by one, as we say. But after
identifying myself with it, I must create an object which resembles the tree.*[2]

Approaching a subject by these methods can form the basis for
idea discovery in any investigative area. The discovery sources
are virtually limitless and include trees, flowers, insects, animal
and bird forms, skeletal structures, machines, markets, buildings,
antiques, magnified creatures, precision instruments, and many,
many other sources from the natural and man-made world. Idea
sources of this type will be fully treated in the following
chapters.

Imagination Is a Key Factor in Developing Artistic Ideas

The acquisition of knowledge is not enough in itself to nour-
ish artistic thoughts. We must take the information that we
have gained through investigation and release it to the magnificent world of our imagination! It is in this realm that data comes
alive and is reborn as an art form. By developing our imaginative
powers, we are able to refine ideas from their rough state and
express them in ways that are unique, original, and aesthetically
satisfying.

Without imagination, the artist would be a mere craftsman.
The artist knows that he must combine both skill and uniqueness

of idea to achieve his aim. Imagination becomes the fuel by
which information is converted into artistic energy and ultimately the art product. From our imagination, we have the
ability to create entirely new images — castles in the sea, phan-
tasies, satires, social comments, new impressions of man, or a
fresh interpretation of the commonplace subjects in our environment. Our imagination enables us to recreate part or all
of the present world, or entirely new worlds of our own!

Where Does the Artist Obtain His Ideas for Art?

Aesthetic form first takes root as a seedling in the imagination where the mind's eye catches the first glimmer, or spark.
The artist manipulates and explores these initial ideas with art
media until the first rough forms are suggested in the material.
Such a release is not something that is culminated at the outset.
There is a groping, probing, experimental process of inquiry.
Sometimes the process is lengthy, other times rapid, always intense, until the artist is able to resolve the ideas through the
final art work.

Many ideas may come to mind but not all reach the point
where they can be developed into visually pleasing statements.
While it is possible to be struck with inspiration, the artist usually starts with rough ideas that he may have been investigating
for days, even months. These rough ideas serve as clues by which
he experiments and searches through an art medium until an
aesthetic toe hold has been established. Each artist develops his
ideas by approaching his work in an individual manner. He may
be influenced by others, and so he should be in order to learn
and gain insights, but he knows that he must carve his own
path through the artistic wilderness.

---

[2]Escholier, Raymond, *Matisse: From the Life*, London: Faber and Faber,
Ltd., 1960.

Ralph Talbert

Imagination can help us
to create all or any part
of the present world.
We may also create
new worlds of our own.

"House by the Railroad," (1925), by Edward Hopper.
Oil on canvas, 24 x 29".
Collection, The Museum of Modern Art, New York.

The following statements will offer some clues into the manner in which several artists search for ideas in their art. Each of the artists listed is influenced by different forces and consequently each reacts personally to his immediate preferences. Some of the artists do not seek subject clues outside of the canvas itself. Others prefer to intellectualize or observe some element of the environment:

Jackson Pollock:

I don't work from drawings or colour sketches. My painting is direct . . . The method of painting is the natural growth of a need. I want to express my feelings rather than illustrate them. Technique is just a means of arriving at a statement. When I am painting I have a general notion as to what I am about. I can control the flow of paint; there is no accident, just as there is no beginning and no end.[3]

Max Beckmann:

A human face, a hand, a woman's breast or a manly body, an expression of conflicting joy and pain, the infinite ocean, savage crags, the melancholy speech of black trees against the snow, the fierce power of spring blossoms and the heavy lethargy of a hot summer noon when our old friend Pan is asleep and the ghosts of noon are murmuring — all this is enough to make us forget the sorrows of the world, or to give them form.[4]

Edward Hopper:

My aim in painting has always been the most exact transcription possible of my most intimate impressions of nature . . . I have tried to present my sensations in what is the most congenial and impressive form possible to me. The technical obstacles of painting perhaps dictate this form. It derives also from the limitations of personality.[5]

Abraham Rattner:

In painting I find that the articulative force is color. Color is to a painting what sound is to music. It is not limited by the color we experience in the objective world, but the experiences of our livingness touch the keys and chords of our inner being and bring into play that wonderful color world of our imagination.[6]

Franz Kline:

I make preliminary drawings, other times I paint directly, other times I start a painting and then paint it out so that it becomes another painting or nothing at all. If a painting doesn't work, throw it out.[7]

Josef Albers:

Sometimes I close my eyes, and slowly certain color ideas begin to take shape. Then I make any number of preliminary sketches — small, and as a rule not of much importance to start with. Gradually, after innumerable tests, experiments, juxtapositions and slight changes, the picture begins to work.[8]

An idea could strike at anytime, anywhere. It could be a part of nature or something constructed by man. The trigger mechanism in the aesthetic experience remains personal and elusive.

[3]Friedenthal, Richard, *Letters of the Great Artists,* New York: Random House, Inc., 1963, page 272.

[4]*Ibid.,* page 215.

[5]University of Minnesota, Department of Art, *40 American Painters, 1940-1950,* 1951, page 33.

[6]Leepa, Allen, *The Challenge of Modern Art,* New York: The Beechhurst Press, 1949, page 197. By permission of A. S. Barnes & Co., Inc.

[7]Kuh, Katherine, *The Artist's Voice,* New York: Harper & Row, 1962, p. 145.

[8]*Ibid.,* pages 20-21.

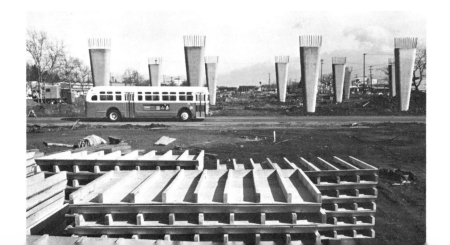

To experience the beginnings of art, one must multiply the ways in which he discovers his world.

Robert Mallary:

> *Prior to coming to New York in 1959 I lived for four years in New Mexico and reacted strongly to the place. The sandy and stone-like surfaces of my paintings and relief panels were influenced by the topography of the area . . . You could rightly infer from this that I like to draw upon what is at hand and identify myself to some degree with the "scene," but at the same time I like to stand somewhat apart and use what I appropriate in my own way.[9]*

Once the artist is able to relate his ideas to a specific material in a manner that satisfies his critical eye, he proceeds to refine the form until he feels nothing further can be stated. It is possible for an artist to successfully complete his message or theme within a single art work. More than likely, he will pursue his thinking in depth through a series of related art works all of which touch on the same theme or idea. To the less experienced eye, it may appear that all of a certain artist's paintings are repetitive because of a consistency of theme. Therefore, it may seem that he is repeating himself unnecessarily. For the artist, however, the minutest variations of a line, shape, color, or image may suggest hundreds of new possibilities for continuing his theme. A single art product is seldom more than the first statement of an idea. Until the artist has expanded the idea through a continued search, with many variations, it usually remains as a temporary statement.

To be an artist means to be fully alive as a person and eager to discover the details of life! To do so, one must give himself completely to the task. The artist is aware of his world and seeks it out rather than waiting for it to beckon him. He reveals this search in his work; sometimes he succeeds, sometimes not. His work usually reveals his tremendous vision of life. Most artists are able to see way beyond the ordinary capacity to understand

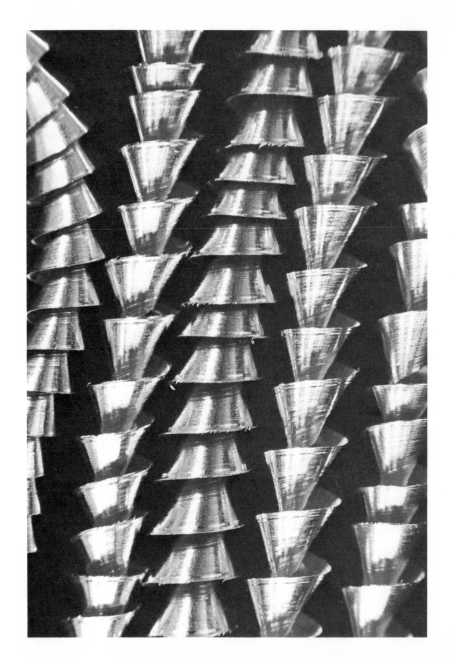

9"Robert Mallary Interviewed," *ARTFORUM,* Vol. II, Number 7, January, 1964, page 37.

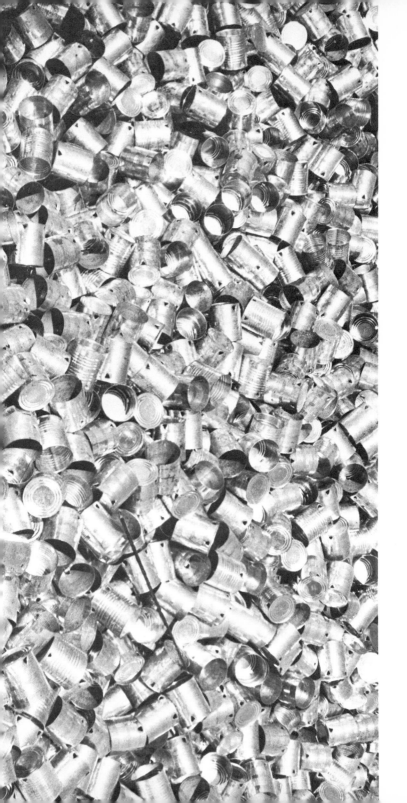

visual delight, for this is their territory. What the philosopher will put into words and phrases, the artist will render with color, line, and tool. The artist is both searcher and discoverer. He is not content to remain with the routine appearance of things, and rather desires to dig deeper to uncover other possibilities for interpreting an idea. By his very nature, the artist does not remain with a static idea of man or thing. He strives to create structure and form from chaos. Creativeness thus becomes his standard.

The following chapters are intended to be stimulating adventures in discovering unusual and unique sources for art ideas. Each of these sources is aimed at encouraging the student of art into further investigation of the source, as well as the pursuit of additional possibilities of his own. It is hoped that through such discoveries, one will develop a uniquely personal manner of structuring forms in both mind and art media.

Ralph Talbert

The forms for art are always there yet remain elusive until we single them out from the milieu and redefine their purposes.

The youth ought first to learn perspective, then the proportions of everything, then he should learn from the hand of a good master in order to accustom himself to good limbs; then from nature in order to confirm for himself the reasons for what he has learnt; then for a time he should study the works of different masters; then make it a habit to practise and work at his art.[1]

Howard Laws

Chapter 2

Sources for Discovering the Human Form

The human figure as a source for art ideas is a wonderful, challenging adventure. Every conceivable sort of aesthetic configuration is there to grip the artist as he grapples with form. Sources of art ideas relating to the figure can be found in most locations. Some especially lucrative sources include markets, shops, and other merchandise centers. Here, the figure can be studied in motion and against various backgrounds. The action of a form bending over a meat counter, or weighing a bag of oranges may trigger a myriad of possibilities for visual exploration. One should bear in mind that any such physical act may appear inconsequential when considered as a fragment of daily routines. However, the artist is able to see such simple routines as weighing fruit with a charge of aesthetic impact! He takes the subject under view and strives to assemble it into a satisfying artistic relationship. The subject per se remains an ordinary experience of life. The artist seeks to take the specific subject and build it from its chaotic moment in space to an aes-

[1]MacCurdy, Edward, (ed.), *Notebooks of Leonardo Da Vinci*, New York: George Braziller, Inc., 1956, page 863. Reprinted from the original MacCurdy volumes published by Reynal and Hitchcock.

thetic achievement with art media. As such, he engages in an expressive act of visual creation.

The Figure in Motion

The figure in action might serve as an interesting source for ideas. The subject could be a carpenter pounding a nail, a fisherman carrying a net, or a lady selling newspapers on a street corner. It might be a butcher chopping meat on a block, or a jeweler inspecting the mechanism in a watch. Any type of atmosphere could spark an entire chain of ideas relative to a selected scene.

If we deal with a figurative subject observed in the darkness of evening, we could consider figures walking through shadows, mist, fog, rain, snow, and the like. We might concentrate more on exaggerated glimpses rather than deliberate details. We could examine the figure running, walking, or pausing. Seeing the figure at night is completely in contrast to daylight viewing. The figure viewed against a backdrop of snow is quite different from a figure in full sunlight on a beach. The figure might be climbing stairs, stepping down from a bus, bending over, or falling. The figure as artistic subject presents no limitations to the imaginative eye. Any action of the figure could be stimulation for a painting, a drawing, a piece of sculpture, or other art material. The subject might be crossing a street, walking in the park, reading a sign in a store window, waiting for a light to change, greeting an old friend, or any other natural motion of the figure. The artist is like a stopwatch in many ways. He records the moment of impact, and goes on to give it his personal twist.

Sports events offer the artist an opportunity to observe figures in combination. Some players are crouched, as in football. Some are caught running at high speed, and some are jumping or being tackled. One can choose to focus on the single individual or examine a cluster of figures in a close play. In games such as football and hockey, the action is often blurred to natural vision because of the rapidity of play, and of blind spots from bunching up of players. Interesting also is the external garb — helmets, spikes, skates, shoulder pads, sweatshirts with eye-catching numbers, and shin guards — all of which lend themselves well to collage type of constructions. In lieu of attendance at such events, television provides a fine substitute for catching the action.

Winter sports such as ice skating and sledding offer opportunities to observe the figure in more graceful motion. Emphasis in this instance is not on speed but on subtlety of human form. The reflections of figures on snow and ice may spur one to examine such subjects more closely. Night time skating may increase the characteristics of reflections and snowy impressions of winter drama.

Figurative Ideas at Close Range

Let's think in terms of the figure as it appears at close range. This means moving in close to observe and sharpen our focus on details. Sometimes the artist has to decide which part of the figure is worth exploring; perhaps the eyes should be the dominant focal point in a composition; or the entire facial section might be a suitable area for emphasis. If so, what would a face look like if it were placed on the canvas so that only the main features occupied the entire picture space? By this same token, one might consider the torso only as the subject for a composition. This has been done often in sculptural media. It might be that the body from the waist up will offer more to a particularly selective eye. Another consideration might be to have the subject's long flowing hair come down across the face. The play of shadows across a cheek, or a certain tilt of a head may

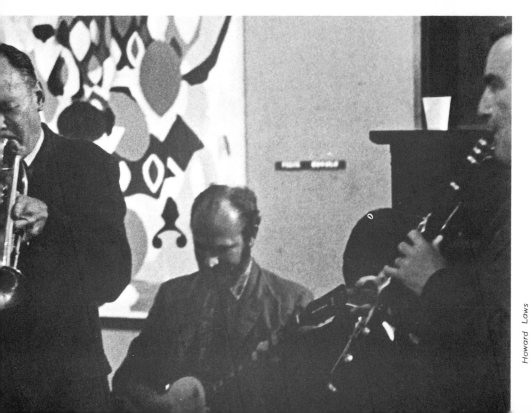

Howard Laws

Through the eyes of the camera we are able to stop a specific motion and bring it into focus for further study.

"Nous Sommes Fous" by George Rouault
Courtesy, Crocker Art Gallery, Sacramento, California

Nuances of the subject can become descriptive expressions of the art work. The lift of a hand or a slight smile can evoke an image that is as lasting as the aesthetic material.

be sufficient to begin the artistic search. One has to be always on the alert for the choice that will move him to begin composing the form in a definite manner.

The artist may wish to bring out the personality of his subject. To do this might suggest many things. What type of person is this? What are the most intriguing qualities of this person? What characteristics are outstanding? How can this subject be brought to an expressive climax? The artist doesn't necessarily aim to illustrate his subject verbatim, but rather to envision it along his own terms.

The artist might conceive the figure much larger than actual size. Enlarging the scale changes the type of response to the subject. It directs one to see the figure in a different light. Working above normal scale can be done with the entire figure or with the face alone, or with any portion of the figure. When we think of figures on a larger-than-life scale, we are more apt to think in terms of being "in the work" as opposed to remaining at our usual emotional distance as viewer. One must consider that Michelangelo's "David" may have been much less impressive had it been of normal scale.

The movies also provide a source of interesting comparison in reference to the large-sized figures which appear on the screen. The gigantic scale of the figure can be both stimulating and valuable as a source for artistic treatment. It isn't often that we see the figure in such heraldic proportions, especially in painting. Mark Rothko's color swatches are much less impressive in slide form. Just imagine the challenges involved in painting a figure ten times life size!

Ideas for handling the art form do not need to exceed natural scale. Art production might also be considered below natural scale. The idea of being able to hold a complete painting in one's palm could be a fascinating conjecture. Just think!

A painting in miniature! The figures on coins, paper money, and pendants might serve as source material in the development of the human form along these lines. One should not overlook the possibility of painting pictures that range from very small to very large. The comparison of paintings which are four inches square with those ten feet tall is an interesting possibility!

Figures in the Crowd

The artist might decide to work with the solitary figure, or he may combine two or more figures in a compositional series. Sometimes an entire painting could consist of several figures. The mere challenge of attempting to relate several figures in a pleasing arrangement excites the imagination. Pieter Brueghel, the famed sixteenth century German artist was a master of the group figure scene.

There are countless source opportunities for obtaining material related to the study of crowds. Sports events are especially good for studying individuals at both close range and from a distance. In placing large numbers of figures in a composition, the artist may choose to handle each figure anonymously or he may work each figure in a meticulously detailed fashion. The players would provide excellent subjects for studying overlapping aspects of objects seen on a moving field. The figures might be rendered with a "blurred" technique to suggest rapid action, or be clearly represented as in a moment of pause. The composite structure of crowds in bleacher and stadium seats offers wonderful studies from various vantage points. There is also the interesting observational position of being close to the ground and studying the action from a low eye level. The artist learns to see the usual in unusual and interesting ways. He goes beyond the ordinary to give us a fresh viewpoint that is moving in both technique and idea.

"Head of Bearded Man" by Peter Paul Rubens
Courtesy, Crocker Art Gallery,
Sacramento, California

In studying the figure at
close range, specific information comes into focus. Points
of emphasis are an individual
thing and must be decided
by the artist.

Indian at Banŏs, Ecuador
Photograph, courtesy of Edward S. Ross, Curator,
California Academy of Sciences,
San Francisco, California

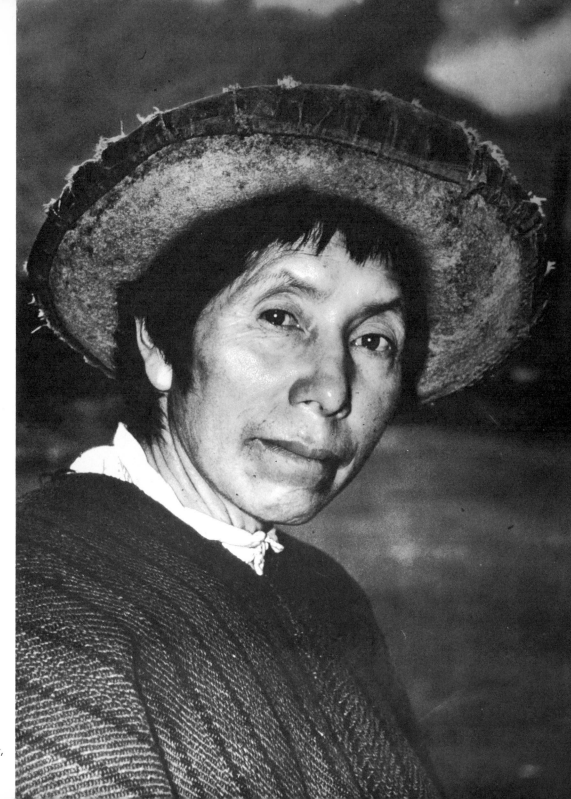

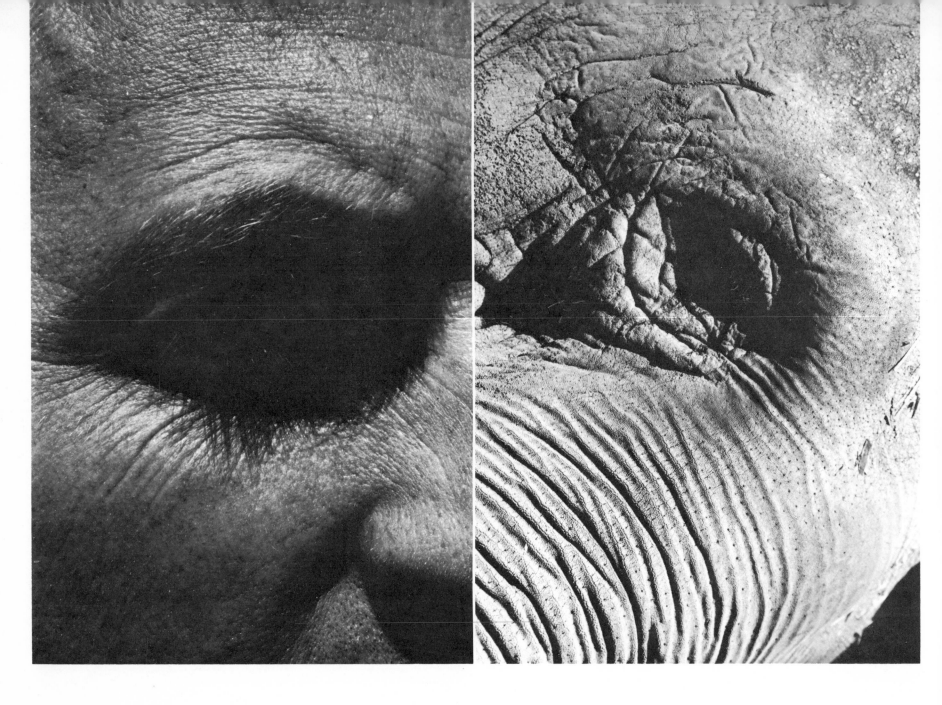

In observation, it is essential to sharpen one's focus, for accurate perception is not always possible at first inspection. Objects which appear to be one thing often turn out to be another.

:retia" by Lucas Cranach
tesy, Crocker Art Gallery,
amento, California

"Romany Girl" by Robert Henri
Courtesy, Crocker Art Gallery,
Sacramento, California

"Motorcycle King" by Earl Linderman

The manner of interpreting a subject always remains highly personal. While the age in which the artist lives influences his manner of working, the result is always an individual accomplishment.

Wm. Paxton Hoag

Rod Commons

Sports events provide the artist with excellent opportunities to study and sketch the figure in motion singly or in groups.

Rod Commons

Vasil Madzelan

"Romans and Orientals in Battle" (probably by) Jorg Breu, the Elder. Courtesy, Crocker Art Gallery, Sacramento, California

Crowd scenes can be excellent aesthetic material. Any location that provides throngs of bustling humanity is appropriate for obtaining ideas. Parades, transportation terminals, and public events are likely sources.

Actually experiencing crowds can be an essential part of understanding what they are like. Walking through a crowded lobby, standing in a jam-packed elevator, waiting in a long line at a box office, or being shoved into a bus can provide the feeling that one wishes to explore. It could be rather exciting to be in such circumstances when one is there intentionally to meet certain artistic objectives.

Beaches and parks are marvelous for offering to the artist an uninhibited cross-section of the various hulks and forms of sun-bathing humanity. The artist may decide to work from a lone figure or incorporate a feeling of teeming masses in his composition. To capture the possibilities in such a subject, it might be challenging to view the individual bathers from a point above while looking straight down. One might view the scene through the crooked elbow of a bather. The characteristic trappings of the bathing beach might be something to study for artistic clues — sunglasses, sun tan lotion, radios, towels, beach umbrellas, sand castles, and ice cream stands. Each artist must bring his particular insight to the subject. Any crowd scene can serve as a jumping-off point for the artist.

The camera can be an extremely important instrument for recording multiple aspects of a subject. When one has only minutes to capture the many images that comprise a subject, means other than normal observation must be employed. With the camera to lend assistance, the artist can move more rapidly and know that he has a record for later selection and consideration as subject material. Even the tiniest details can be captured by the sharp-eyed individual who sees possibilities in the most unlikely combinations.

A political convention is an opportune situation for observing the high-pitched excitement of a group. It is generally a colorful, exciting scene, and provides many chances for compositional material in the form of patriotic colors, placards, ticker tape, and just plain smothered humanity. Clues for this type of subject can be extracted from magazines, newsreels, and television.

Other sources for crowds, color, and excitement include parades with marching figures in uniform, musical instruments, decorated horses, old-time cars, and jumping clowns; the circus is an especially challenging subject when one thinks of the trapeze, balancing acts, wild animals, cages, and the high-powered, glittering excitement of the show.

Railroad terminals are fascinating places for ideas. One views the endlessly-long waiting benches thronged with souls, some on the way to nowhere. Another source of artistic material are the crowd scenes of our busy streets. The visual backdrop of store fronts, signs, neon, and moving traffic offers stimulating possibilities, especially when one thinks of collage, and painting. The artist who observes these various scenes and events should be turning them over in his mind with an eye to how he will transform specific aspects into compositional material. In this respect, the artist has to see the potential in a subject. It is not necessary that he always record it in a representational fashion. Far from such a notion, for the inventive artist will take the scene and run with it until he makes a breakthrough that satisfies him in terms of his own critical standard.

The Seated Figure as Subject Potential

We might consider the human form in a variety of seated positions as a source of aesthetic discovery. In the beginning, we may consider the number of variations in position that a person might assume while seated. For example, seated positions include sitting erect or slouched, leaning on one's elbow, sitting with head sloped downward, reading a book, holding a child, resting one's hand under the chin or against the nose,

"Nymphs Bathing" by William Adolphe Bouguereau
Courtesy, Pioneer Museum and Haggin Galleries, Stockton, California

"Apollo and the Muses" by Francesco Solimena
Courtesy, Crocker Art Gallery, Sacramento, California

"Denial" by Ken Morrow
Courtesy, Crocker Art Gallery,
Sacramento, California

Treatment of the figure in groups has been a powerful theme for the artist of every age. Expression ranges from the lyrical to the abstract.

"Four Heads" by Theodore Rousseau
Courtesy, Crocker Art Gallery,
Sacramento, California

The beach offers massive doses of humanity that are ideal for interpretation. Close ups as well as distant action provide various aesthetic considerations.

and countless variations. The visual appearance of the seated figure varies rapidly when we alter the seat itself. The body relates to the supporting structure in terms of the design and surface hardness of the seating structure. As such, the body also varies in position when the supporting structure changes — a park bench, a sofa, a bathtub, bleachers at a sporting event, an automobile seat, a theatre seat, a restaurant booth, a porch swing, a horse.

Further variation of the seated figure as a subject for art includes the atmospheric conditions relevant to the subject. We might consider the subject under artificial light, at dawn, at early evening, at dark, or in bright sunlight. The play of shadows and light across the subject can be fascinating indeed. The features of the face might be handled in great detail or remain a subtle suggestion in the form of a darkened eye socket and cheekbone in profile; or the curl of a lip may become evident as the subject moves from shadows toward full light. The figure in the act of doing simple, ordinary functions can trigger various possibilities for aesthetic considerations. The subject might be seated at a table and engaged in eating, or playing cards (one thinks of Cezanne's "Cardplayers"). We might relate to a subject seated at her dressing table combing her hair. The commonplace actions of the figure in personal habits, such as drying oneself after a bath, dressing, or climbing into bed might suggest possibilities for the artist's subtle hand. Auguste Renoir, Edward Hopper, Andrew Wyeth, and many others have successfully used the common experiences of living as their subject matter.

We might also consider the seated subject as he appears in public, on a bus, behind a cash register, behind a teller's window at the bank, or selling tickets in a theatre box office.

The viewing position which the artist selects should be an important factor in studying the subject for a drawing, painting, or other type of art production. The artist should seek new and surprising means for composing his pictures. Placing the figure at close range and cutting it abruptly, as well as placing the figures at diagonals present more stimulating suggestions in figure treatment. Looking directly up from below, or down from above, or observing the subject from an extremely close range offer more interesting insights for the interpretation of the human form. The study of any subject for that matter should be undertaken in a similar fashion. The artist should make it one of his first aims to see his subject with an originality and freshness of vision. In this manner, his work is more likely to sparkle as visual and interpretative phenomena.

Ideas for the Figure in Repose

Thinking of the figure from the reclining position can suggest interesting ideas to consider for aesthetic purposes. The figure might be in any position of recline or degree of slope. The figure might be observed in a hammock, on a bed, a couch, in the grass, on a bench at a train station, or in a hospital bed. Each supporting structure might suggest a different type of pose for the individual figure. The thought of using a couch for a figurative support and backdrop suggests various considerations. The couch, for instance, could be elaborately decked with a velvety material and ornately carved legs; or it might be old, over-stuffed and dusty. When Henri Matisse, the French artist worked with the figure in a reclining pose, he was very much concerned with the couch and the surrounding background subjects. He decorated and embellished the area around the model while treating the model quite simply, thus creating a beautiful contrast between active and quiet areas in his com-

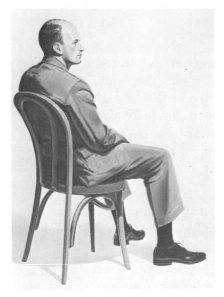

Ralph Talbert

"Man in Blue Chair" by Wayne Thiebaud
Courtesy, Crocker Art Gallery,
Sacramento, California

Howard Laws

The seated figure can offer much in the way of aesthetic consideration. The range of interpretation is infinite and limited only by the skill of the artist.

Howard Laws

Drawing by Robert Henri
Courtesy, Crocker Art Gallery,
Sacramento, California

Figure study by C. Venard
Courtesy, Crocker Art Gallery,
Sacramento, California

"St. George and the Dragon I" by Albrecht Durer
Courtesy, Crocker Art Gallery, Sacramento, California

"La Coiffure" by Auguste Renoir
Courtesy, Pioneer Museum and Haggin Galleries,
Stockton, California

positions. There are many well-known "couch" paintings: one thinks of Manet's "Olympia" and Ingres's "Odalisque with a Slave."

We might deal with more unusual sources for composing a picture; a lonely figure slumped in a deserted doorway on an old street, or a figure soaking in a bathtub with magazine in hand; or a stuffy old wing chair in a darkened parlor, or a figure lying on a back lawn of flowers, the sun creating a dancing pattern across the form. All of these sources and many more can be discovered through observation of actual and recorded subjects.

Figurative Sources in the Environment

Television can be a stimulating source of visual information. One should turn the volume down so that only the visual image is apparent. This allows us to focus on the motion without the distraction of sound.

Mannequins in store windows and on counters have a very special life of their own; motionless, yet fixed in a perpetual gaze that permits the artist to return as often as necessary. The pseudo-image also provides a variation to the live subject. The inventive artist might see new directions for using the mannequins as subject material. The possibilities of actually incorporating the mannequin as part of sculptural material have already been employed by several contemporary artists, i. e. Marisol, Keinhŏlz, etc. The entire mannequin might be employed or fragments of it, as part of a sculptural piece. Recent artists have also taken to changing the appearance of the mannequin by painting on it and otherwise modifying the surface form.

Another type of mannequin in reduced form is the doll. The artist might see fresh possibilities in such a motionless, but ani-

mated structure. The elaborate construction of dolls with their moving eyes and mouth parts, as well as mechanical voices might suggest new worlds to the artist.

Related to this source is the entire range of toys, models, and plaster images created for commercial consumption. While most are common and trite if we think of their surface appearance, the artist may be able to see new directions for shaping and extending their particular imagery. One must keep in mind that in artistic production, realistic expression is only one of countless ways to say "figure," and each way is dependent on the choice and method of the artist.

Biological specimens of skeletons might be an interesting source of figurative material. The skeletal structure would enable the artist to start from the basic foundation and build an image in any direction that he decides will make an artistic statement.

Magazine photographs allow an unending supply of figures in various poses. An advantage of the magazine model is that it can be cut up and altered to create striking effects and approaches. Faces can be placed on other bodies, and new forms for the torso can be suggested. Montages, collages, and experimentation with overlapping techniques and pasting can release new sources for artistic consideration. Eyes, noses, and bodily appendages can be transposed and joined in new relationships for figurative subjects.

The artist essentially gives new dimensions to a specific form. He attempts a fresh approach to a subject. For example, the artist might compare the similarities and differences between the human form and that of other vertebrates. Some questions to explore along this line might include the following:

Jon Geil

lls" by Gary Pruner
tesy, Crocker Art Gallery, Sacramento, California

Jon Geil

In terms of idea potential, almost any subject in the environment can become electric for the searching eye. Dolls and mannequins are especially fruitful for figurative variations. Antique shops offer a wealth of material.

What are the similarities of an eye in man, animal, frog, bird, and insect?

How do the jaw and mouth parts differ between man and animal? Between man and insect?

Is there a similarity between fingers and paws? Fingers and claws?

Art museums provide a marvelous collection of human form down through history. The artist is able to compare various interpretations of the figure throughout the evolution of man. He can study the paintings of the cave man, and those who followed to see how the artist, influenced by religious and tribal beliefs, interpreted the human form. The works of contemporary artists should also be studied to gain source ideas and insights. One never grows sufficiently if one remains within himself and waits for something to happen. The artist, like all of us, needs outside stimulation in great quantities in order to extend his own boundaries.

Unusual Discovery Sources for the Figure

It is also possible to form new figurative relationships through exploration of art media. De Kooning developed a new way to say "woman" through inventive processes with paint. Such unconventional approaches to the use of composition and pigment manipulation often disturb us by their very unorthodoxy.

Found objects might be arranged to suggest the human form. Disguising the figure by putting a stocking over the face or applying theatrical make-up can suggest aesthetic directions. Imaginative light sources can create wonderful dramatic aspects through shadow distortion and exaggeration.

Studying figures through the opposite end of binoculars, and also close-up observation of figures through binoculars allow the observer to come close without detection to observe details. Medical diagrams and X rays which show the inside and bony aspects of the human form provide viewpoints in transparency which give the artist an opportunity to see the form in a fresh manner. Some medical equipment can record part or all of the human form by light pattern and electrical impulse. Investigating sources of this nature can throw new insights into the study of the human form. Recent experiments with sound patterns which transform impulses into a visual image might suggest a direction for exploring the figure from a more unusual viewpoint. Another approach to the figure might deal with the actual creation of a new figurative type. That is, the artist may modify the human form to fit an aesthetic structure of his choice. In this type of approach to the figure, many arms and legs are possible. The form can be distorted as well. In a sense, the artist creates a fresh view of the human form. Another instance in which a new vehicle for expressing "figure" can be developed may relate to the subject of man as an idea in abstraction, devoid of present concepts of form. In this case, the thoughts, actions, previous experiences and "a felt presence" may be composed to suggest a visual interpretation; or we might think of a figure without the "skin." This would expose the muscles and present a fresh source of possibility. We might also consider the figure in a transparent state, in which other subjects can appear and be combined into and through the form. We might also consider the figure as a subject that fades and becomes vague, or has properties which allow the form to change, such as a stretching or elongated appearance. Examples of this sort are clearly evident in the works of El Greco who elongated his figures, and Chagall, who rubberized the form to achieve dreamy qualities of flight.

More unusual aspects of a subject can be obtained by observing at close range as well as in the distance. Night viewing offers aspects not available in full light.

Ralph Talbert

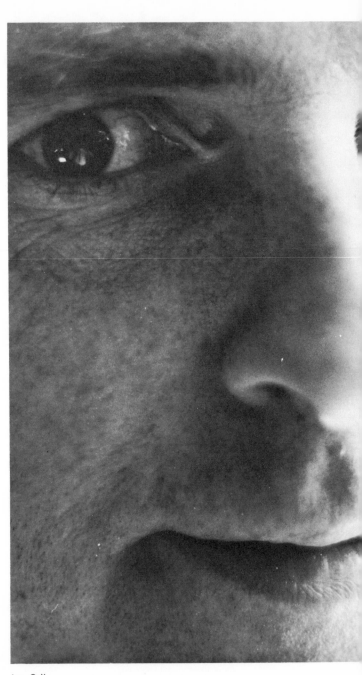

Jon Geil

Jon Geil

Nick DeLucia

Searching for more unusual details of a subject can open doorways to new insights for art expression.

Enlargement of a cribbage board.

Jon Geil

The Figure in Uniform

Another fruitful idea source relates to figures that come under the category of public service in one capacity or another. All of these subjects wear labels and are members of various professional, semi-professional, and skilled groups. In one group are the uniformed legions of box office personnel, change girls, ticket takers at public events, and cashiers who peer out from behind ringing cash machines. Another group of uniformed service people includes waiters, busboys, bellhops and doormen. One associates them with serving trays, dishes, elevators, suitcases, and dining parlors, all of which can suggest idea material for an art work.

Another possibility along this line includes the uniformed protective agencies in the service of our local, state, and federal government. This group includes city policemen, sheriff's deputies, state police, and the federal branches of the service including the Army, Navy, Marines, and Air Force. One source of visual stimulation might be to focus on the identifying symbols of the group, such as the badge, the helmet, and the weapons. The significance of the uniform itself as a symbolic statement may suggest more to the artist than the anonymous individual who wears it. In this instance, we might expand on the symbolic interpretation by exaggerating the badge, helmet, stripes, boots, and protective implements. This type of approach could be employed with other groups also. A group that includes many specialties, and may be considered as beneficial to society is composed of doctors, dentists, technicians, and scientists. These individuals wear the white smock — a symbol of cleanliness. The white smock also serves bakers, butchers, grocery clerks, beauty salon operators, and so forth. Another symbolic uniform, and a contrast to the purity of the white smock, is the black leather trappings of the motorcyclist, and of some teenage gangs. In this instance, the black jacket evokes a negative response. "Black" becomes synonymous with hard-boiled, tough guy operations. One other group may suggest possibilities for aesthetic performance. This includes the less fortunate members of our society — the derelicts and transients, the unwanted, stubble-bearded dregs of society who normally occupy the riverfront sections of our larger cities. Their uniforms are not shiny and polished, yet we recognize such members by their tattered attire. Surely, the artist can be moved to respond artistically in such an environment.

The uniforms that people wear are a form of identification. Uniforms can represent almost anything from conformity to courage, and the artist can explore the entire gamut of possibilities.

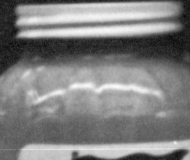

The Signs and Symbols
of the City

Chapter 3

Man has created cities to house both himself and his implements and has developed a prodigious array of imaginative and visually fascinating machines, tools, and structures. The products of such collective genius offer an untold wealth of ideas before the talents of the artist. He has but to select from this jungle of man-made images those forms which can excite and move him to create new images of his own.

In the process of constructing civilized society, current items replace worn models, so that a continuous treadmill removes parts which no longer serve man. Some remnants are cast by the wayside or are thrown carelessly on a pile of discards. Still others cling desperately in their last gasping usefulness. Rarer still are those objects which are restored and given a new birth under the heading, "Antiques." The residue of life's erosion is evident everywhere. The products of man rust, decay, age, wear out, and deteriorate. The

[1]Giorgio de Chirico, from Friedenthal, Richard, *Letters of the Great Artists*, New York: Random House, Inc., 1963, page 233.

51

process of destruction is gradual, however, and the sensitive eye can discover unlimited possibilities for inventing unusual forms to express beauty. Some materials peel or flake, as painted surfaces; others rust or oxidize, as iron or copper. Still others, such as wood, decay. The elements of nature continue their corrosive action, and when it is complete, both natural forms and the forms of man are changed. The artist who has original vision learns to take note of these changes in his search for unique and original images.

Buildings, an Unfolding Drama of Life

Buildings which have weathered the elements for years on end are visually pleasing in terms of their exterior surfaces. Wooden structures are especially interesting for their bleached woods which have braved the sun and wind continuously. These structures often yield a rich visual treasury of gray, white, and patterned surfaces. Buildings of this nature can be found in many portions of a city, but more often than not they are disappearing before the coming storm of contemporary architecture. Barns along the highways still offer a tremendous variety of beautifully bleached and rotted lumber. One can sense the stories which lie resting within their decayed walls.

To the less sensitive eye, corroded surfaces imply a necessary replacement when funds become available. To the artist, weathered buildings are a symbol of past history, and visual evidence of the beauty that can be found in places not usually considered beautiful.

A more detailed examination of an old structure can reveal pockets of exquisite delight to the eye. One might begin at the front gate. It could be wooden or wrought iron in character. It may squeak when opened. There may be a definite pattern to the gate construction. The weathering effects may produce interesting textural relationships. Check the sidewalk or pathway as you move toward the house. The cement or stone slabs may be stained and colored. The greens and tans of grasses can produce a subtle charm on bleached concrete. As you reach the house, be alert for stained glass in the windows, decorative cornices at the top of the columns and around the roof line. Study the shape of the entire structure from a short distance off. When close to the building, look up at the second story. Be alert to the width and design of the windows. Are there any old lace curtains at the windows? Is the glass intact? Check for old furniture on the porch, and for a well in the yard. Can you detect any square nails in the wood? Are there any spindles in the porch rail? Are they pleasing in shape? As you move around to the back of the structure, note the type of foundation, whether or not there is a storm cellar, and whether there are peeling paint patterns on the side walls. Be alert for any flowers in bloom on the property. Moving inside the structure would open up a vast range of possibilities. Pertinent items to consider for visual appeal include the staircase, the ceilings, any outcropping posts or supporting beams, the fireplace, tattered wallpaper, electrical fixtures, and whatever else might be stimulating as source material. An artist immediately realizes that any fragment of the existing situation could serve as raw material for a painting or other type of art work. The things that move different people may be quite different in character — the pattern of the fireplace bricks, coated with years of black soot and ash; a wooden cupboard in the pantry with its crude drawers and empty, grimy shelves; an entire wall with its old pictures, torn wallpaper, and cobwebs that stretch across the corners.

Often, buildings in the old sections of town that are still in operation present such a slightly decayed image as well as the feeling for present usefulness. Dingy, poorly lighted, with old tables and chairs, and dark drapes that hold a musty scent, the smell of thousands of plates of food and coffee — all these impressions stir the observant artist.

The pulse of the city is everywhere and the artist can find points of discovery by searching out various sources. Shops that carry old as well as new merchandise can suggest possibilities for interpretation into art media.

Buildings can suggest many possibilities for artistic relationships. The exterior as well as the interior should be studied for usable material. Examining specific parts may suggest ideas — worn steps, boarded doorways, peeling surfaces.

Kennedy Mine, Jackson, California
Photographs by Ralph Talbert

Vestiges of history remain throughout the land as evidence of what has gone before. The mine structures and tailing wheels of the gold rush days offer exciting visual material for exploration.

Antique Shops Are Something Special

Many stimulating art ideas are often suggested while exploring out of the way shops and stores. Echoes of life gone before reverberate endlessly in the collections of odds and ends which once served humanity. The objects are often worn at the corners and edges and suggest many past years of joyful use. Many items are stacked one on the other and are topped by several layers of dust. In this fashion, they sleep their dusty sleep, disturbed only by an occasional finger smudge. Antique dealers are masters at collecting and sorting out the residue of past generations. Their collections offer the most varied of merchandise in an assortment of items from many periods and of diverse style and quality. It is not unusual to see contemporary items resting silently with those that date back a century or more. Within such shops, one might find hand-carved pieces of furniture, dishware, glass of varied descriptions, horse-driven wagons, grandfather clocks, rusted implements, farm machinery, old posters, stuffed birds, paintings, gilded frames, lost keys, old books, and hundreds of other items that once served a definite function. Often, the haphazard groupings of such objects can be sufficient to generate a line of exploration. Some shops are literally crammed to the ceiling with an enormous assortment of collected pieces. Just imagine the potential in a room that is completely filled with items from the past. Your childhood, your parents' childhood, and your grandparents' childhood may be there — stored in the closet of centuries. An interesting aspect of antique objects is the variation in styling and design; such a selection could never be found in a contemporary shop. One can visualize a myriad of compositional directions in which to explore. Assemblage, collage, surrealism, and the entire gamut of visual possibility is laid bare before the selective eye of the artist.

Stores, Shops, and Markets

The shops and stores of the city are gilded with a thousand jewels of merchandise to caress the searching eye. Aesthetically speaking, all is not sugar and spice for the artist. It becomes necessary to sort out and select from the vast, chaotic storehouses those pieces of manufactured and natural objects that will offer potential. Each artist becomes his own judge of what he will term useful for idea material. No single object can be omitted from the assortment, if this were possible, for every scrap or tidbit may serve to spark the flame of at least one artist. The city is alive and throbbing with the raw material of artistic creation. From every corner to every off-street shop, the artist can be tempted to search and discover.

Lamp shops offer an adventure in multiple transparencies, prismatic stimulation, whirls of colored glass, and the glow of a countless army of incandescent lamps. Daytime viewing in a lamp shop provides an opportunity to study the shapes and appearances of the lamps. One can observe long, slender shafts, short, vase-like shapes, classically derived structures, porcelain effects, pseudo-early American, hanging lamps evocative of Spanish lanterns, old English styles, and many other mixed breeds that have no specific labels. In the evening hours, the lamps assume a dressier character. There is a warm softness about the lamp shops at dark. The oranges and reds beckon the aesthetic searcher to come closer and drink more deeply of these man-made wonders. The effects of color upon color, and light upon light give one a feeling of being among the stars. Some lights are steady, while others go on and off with mechanical regularity. The visual pattern changes continually and the artist must be ready to capture the beauty that is there.

A bakery shop can be a source of many compositional possibilities. The thick, creamy frostings of cakes and cookies remind

Surfaces which are in a state
of deterioration offer excellent
textural cues. Messages of
past events take on surreal-
istic undertones.

Jon Geil

one of the painter's palette in which thick globules of pigment await the master hand. The filled, creamy delights of doughnuts, turnovers, strudel, creampuffs, and other caloric mountains of sweet, sugary bliss rest in rank upon rank, column by column, stacked endlessly on trays that look out from their bakery shelf at salivating humanity. The baked goodies in fact, become symbolic of society in general. Each doughnut represents a figure, and each figure stands in line, waiting to be counted.

A candy counter can be a splendid source of sparkling color drops amid heaping mounds of textural chocolate surprises. Most candy is basically round in shape and related in overall appearance. Hence, large curvilinear forms merge with countless small crescents and ovals to create a multitude of repetition in the round. Each shape is wed to a primary color and is a visually palatable morsel. For the artist, the candy counter can suggest a magic land festooned with lollipop trees, chocolate bunnies, marshmallow mountains, carrot candy hors d'oeuvres, and cities full of peppermint striped flowers and houses. On the other hand, such goodies can become social commentary for the artist who sees them as a symbol of the inner decay and flabbiness of civilization; an electronic age's frenzied opiate smothered in a sea of custard and coconut cream.

Investigating a coin shop can suggest many new directions for exploration. While coins are extremely interesting to view, their size often discourages all but a cursory glance. If one will pause to examine such coins as he may discover in a shop, he will be more than amply rewarded. There are engraved designs of all sorts, and the coins come from all over the world. American "Liberties" are especially pleasing in coin form. The liberty lady is found walking, standing, and seated depending on the coin and year of mintage. Many popular figures of government including the presidents are clearly stamped on the obverse side of the coins. Numerals of various sizes, styles, and descriptions are pleasingly represented on all coins. Paper money also has an intriguing appeal quite apart from its monetary implications. Foreign currency of this sort is especially interesting to view because of the calligraphic and other symbolic devices. From the standpoint of design or composition, one might consider the enlargement of coined impressions to the scale of a large painting. Enlarging the coin or paper currency emblem to such extreme proportions would change the impression completely. The complete emblem or original design for the coin or currency need not be used. Portions of it, or interpretations based on a fresh direction might be effective. Banners, eagles, stars, and any of the other symbols used on coins may serve to quicken the hand of the artist.

Music stores have a special rhythm for the idea tracker. There are instruments of precise design and construction to attract the observing eye. Musical instruments are a treat to behold; their surfaces glisten and reflect the beat of life around them. When presented in combination, they become a study in contrasting forms and varying thrusts of metal and wood. The finger attachments are particularly arresting as vivid accents to an otherwise streamlined surface. Many instruments have an almost bizarre appearance with their twisting and curling tubes and apertures. Music stands, the cases for the instruments, and sheet music contribute to the total effect. Very fine paintings indeed can be created from a study of musical instruments.

Food markets contain butcher counters that are filled with cuts of red meat in various shapes and tones. The freezer usually has halved carcasses of beef and pork hanging unceremoniously from ominous hooks. The vegetable counters are a joy to the eye. One can find varying examples of circular and free flowing forms, and row after row of greenery; and the greens all have a slightly different cast. Here and there a red, red radish breaks the profusion of green. Subtle purples in the

Jon Geil

Selected viewing in antique shops, grocery stores, and other commercial establishments can result in many ideas for artistic purposes.

"Boston Cremes" by Wayne Thiebaud
Courtesy, Crocker Art Gallery, Sacramento, California

form of egg plants, and the yellows of corn on the cob give a balance to the groupings. The oranges, grapefruit, and lemons are stacked high, and the yellows and oranges dominate the bins, broken only by the soft smack of the limes. Of course, vegetable and fruit counters change their coats with the seasons, and early summer brings berries galore to the market. Baskets of blue, juicy huckleberries abound, often surrounded by strawberries and raspberries. The colors of fresh fruit are brilliant if we think in terms of a painting. We might relate to the idea of fruit as a splash of pure pigment without the more academic limitations of illustration in the conventional approach to the subject.

Cranes, Bulldozers, and Other Steel Monsters

Another source for ideas can be discovered at the various sites where new structures are transforming the landscape. The skeletons of steel, reinforced concrete, and glass offer the investigator precision of line, transparency, and repetition of shape. In their unfinished state, these superstructures stand as giant monsters, poised and silent. Not to be overlooked are the various pieces of heavy earth moving equipment that are an essential part of any construction site. Close observation of a power shovel will reveal its enormous, hinged mouth which swallows huge clods of earth in tremendous bites. In many ways, it reminds one of prehistoric creatures which may have roared and bellowed in a similar fashion. Giant wheels dig into the earth and grinding motors roar their sounds as long appendages swing around to position girders. Some cranes are large enough to lift construction material several stories high. These enormous machines, coupled with their smaller helpers provide many opportunities to observe hinged parts in motion, and to study the action of objects which are gigantic in scale.

Motor vehicles provide interesting contrasts when comparisons are made between the high-powered precision of sports cars and the lumbering bulkiness of trucks. Inspection of the undersurface of huge highway trucks will disclose many fascinating parts including tanks, tubes, hoses, and nozzles. Sports cars project their appearance through dramatic styling and curvilinear rhythms. While the design attributes of the sports car appear more obvious, one must explore deeper in order to discover the aesthetic qualifications of the truck. Often, a small detail of an auto or truck can become quite a fascinating possibility for ideas. Consider as subject material for an art work the dashboard instruments, the steering wheel and related parts, the wheels, the frame of the undersurface, the tail light sections, the gear shift mechanisms, and whatever else may strike a responsive chord in the process of searching for subject data.

Wrecking yards are full of the remnants of old vehicles and serve to offer a picture of machines that no longer serve any function. In a yard of this sort, cars have been stripped down, shorn, mangled, and otherwise eviscerated. As a result, there is often a macabre image that is produced. Front sections are intertwined with frames and fragments of tail gates. Rusted steel is thrust upon a constantly expanding web of metallic waste, as the stockpile of automotive discards rises across the landscape. Some autos have been burned and charred, and present an alarming scene. In many ways, these auto graveyards tell us something of life and death, beginnings and endings for all things.

A visit to the site of the historic steam locomotive is an excellent means of discovering new forms. These huge iron-jawed machines are a fascinating combination of connections and couplings. Their size alone is awesome; and there is nothing so black as a locomotive with its accompanying coal car. Who has ever stood next to one of these beautiful hissing monsters

Trains, cranes, and other steel
monsters combine gears, pul-
leys, mud and steam into a
composite of aesthetic delight
for the sensitive eye. Building
sites and motor pools for
heavy equipment are good
sources to stimulate thinking
of this sort.

and not experienced a tremor of excitement? Old trains are like early cars in many ways. For example, both are devoid of contemporary "streamlining." That is, there are no superimposed speed lines to give the visual illusion of speed. Instead, each section of the engine has a craftsmanlike quality; an individually hand-forged appearance that gives it a feeling of being sculptured. Each part of the engine is individually interesting as a form in itself. Consider the wheels which are enormous in size and weight. Study the braking system. Check the head lamp mechanism. The cab window with its access ladder might suggest possibilities. The barrel vaulting of the main shaft itself is striking as a curving form in space. The front section of the engine with its cow catcher jutting magnificently in front is a stirring sight. One must look at such a locomotive with aesthetic considerations in mind, however. Otherwise, it would be very simple to dismiss the entire experience as a confrontation with an outdated, outmoded assemblage of scrap iron. The artistic personality would never consider such an absurd thought.

If we raise the hood of our automobile, we reveal a composition of steel parts, connecting wires, spark plugs, fan belts, hoses, and cables. Their functions in terms of engine operation is secondary to the bizarre appearance of the entire motor unit which provides a refreshing change to what we are accustomed to viewing in an automobile. Shops that deal with mechanical repairing, such as garages and service stations provide many sources for visual stimulation. The tools that mechanics use are quite interesting when taken as single units. When seen in combination, they present an exciting display of curves, repetitive patterns, and mechanisms. The hydraulic lift used in raising automobiles has a certain attraction with its highly greased shaft and ski-wing appendages. The miscellaneous collection of tool kits, tools, and repairing supplies in such places can serve to trigger many compositional possibilities.

Amusement Centers and Playlands

Amusement centers and playlands are tremendous sources of human energy and excitement. A carnival type of setting permeates these communities and the air is scented with the sounds and smells of roller coasters, ferris wheels, cotton candy, popcorn, stuffed animals, trinket hawkers, food peddlers, and other enticements that are part of such gay establishments. There is a tinsel glitter about such places and the entire scene moves in one giddy whirl. More seasonal versions of this type are the carnivals and the circus. Here we have the side-show attractions which include the abnormalities of man and beast as well as the more gawdy and borderline aspects of the human community. All in all, the carnival, circus, or other type of amusement center is a funny, happy place to go. There is amusement for all ages. For those who like the carnival rides or those who prefer the wheels of fortune, there is something for everyone. And the artist can move freely through the thick of it, sketching, observing, and remembering.

The circus is an especially fruitful source for the artist. Consider as aesthetic potential the big-top ring, the aerialist on the high trapeze, the balancing acts, prancing horses, clowns, the arena, wild animals, popcorn peddlers, magicians, side-show barkers, and hundreds of delighted spectators; and don't forget the brass band. Several artists of the present and recent past incorporated the circus theme into their work. Worth mentioning in this respect are Honoré Daumier and Henri de Toulouse-Lautrec, Pablo Picasso, Paul Klee, and Ben Shahn.

Signs and Billboards: Visual Communication of Our Time

Outdoor advertisements in the form of store front signs, billboards on roof tops and hill tops, window lettering, and the hundreds of free-standing hamburger, gasoline, hardware, and

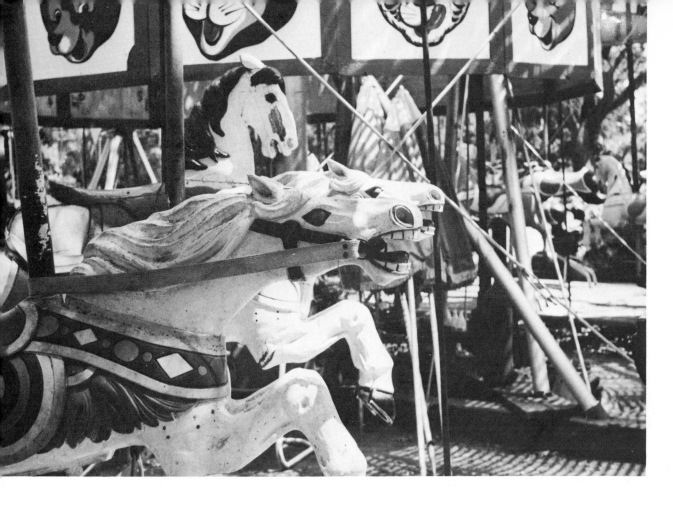

Playlands and amusement centers offer a melange of colors, sounds, sights, and surroundings that cry for interpretation. In such locations the bizarre is commonplace and the tempo is accelerated.

Don Herberholz

"Roseland" by Jack Ogden
Courtesy, Crocker Art Gallery, Sacramento, California

Billboards and other signs can become source material for exploration. The impact of the printed message can become a powerful statement in aesthetic terms.

what-have-you signs form a considerable portion of the contemporary urban landscape. The outdoor message has become the visual signpost in communicating to the often bewildered public the thousands and thousands of man-made products that are offered for sale in one form or another. There are, in fact, signs in such profusion that they tend to cancel each other out. Most of us try to shut out this type of visual experience unless we need to locate something. If we look toward this collection of outdoor media with a sensitive eye to its potential, we are able to transform the chaos before us into plausible working relationships on canvas. Often it is the very unselective grouping of advertisements that forms the nucleus for artistic expression. On many corners in cities across the country, one is able to find a congested mishmash of signs wedged together in a totally shameless display of their product messages. Within this web of visual confusion, the artist should search for the forms that will become aesthetic potential. Actually, the crowding and unselective lumping of the signs makes for wonderful collage ideas or for overlapping suggestions of varied forms. The artist could take some photographs of several corners and other interesting aspects of the signboard world and put his ideas together at a later time in the studio. While one might pull back from this sort of subject matter, it is in fact the banal aspect of the subject that has prompted several contemporary artists to explore this realm.

The effects of darkness and neon lighting add an interesting touch to the scene. At dark, many details are lost and the gawdier aspects are softened by the shadows of night. The neon has a blare of its own, however, and the artificial characteristics of the structures echo strongly. Some signs contain only lettering while others are elaborately structured and include figures, animation, and changing pictures. These range from giant hotdogs dripping with mustard to apple pies, hamburgers, milkshakes, beverages, and utilitarian goods.

Billboards are fascinating in respect to their size. Getting up close to one offers many rewarding observations. The scale becomes so large that original intent is forgotten. This forces us to see the details which are present. That is, we may focus on a watch worn by the painted figure; or an eye that may be two feet wide. When scale is so large, our manner of interpretation is apt to change. The billboard can offer a fresh manner of seeing the subject.

Vehicles of Transportation

Transportation terminals can offer much to the artist in the way of stimulating source material. They are especially exciting when we are not concerned with the pressures of traveling and can concentrate on the arrivals and departures of others.

The airport is fascinating to visit. It is always congested with airplanes landing, taking off, taxiing around the runway, or discharging and loading passengers. The sounds of these huge planes can be exhilarating to say the least. The airport is quite unlike any other place in the city for the big sound of engines, the miracle of flight, and for observing giant craft in motion. Listening to and watching as the pilot warms up the engines can be a moving experience. Another possibility for aesthetic ideas with aircraft is to observe the gayly decorated and painted surfaces. Most smaller craft are beautifully decked in primary colors of red, yellow, and blue with sprinkles of pure white for accent. Aircraft have a special polished appearance that is refreshing to view. They present a bird-like exterior that suggests the element of flight, and one might consider this quality as a possible source for investigation. Other source material could include visual details such as whirring propellers, instrument panels, insignia, tail sections; multiple imagery in relation to aircraft, such as diagonal and crisscross patterns of runways, control towers, blinking signal systems, crowded hangars, and the terminal with its baggage counter, ticket offices, and streaming humanity.

Ocean liners, tugboats, fishing craft and sailboats — vessels that are wed to the water with its richness of color, splash of tide, and reflective qualities — all these are very much a part of an artist's vision in working with boats. These ships of various sorts have a good deal to offer the artist in his investigation. Some items to think about in composing ideas relating to ships and the sea include the exterior form of the craft, the masts, funnels, anchors, driving mechanisms, gears, cabins, portholes, life boats, sailing rigging, rudders, guide lines, and other paraphernalia. The related elements of sky, water, docks, wharves, harbors, and fishing shelters contribute to make such a subject a thrilling experience for the artist.

Train stations and train yards contain intricate networks of tracks, switches, signal systems, freight cars, engines, electrical conductors, steam, smoke, hissing sounds, giant wheels, whistles, lanterns, sidings, depots, and hundreds of other magnificent sources for exploration. Old train depots are grimy with age, and dark from smoke, weather and time. Nevertheless they are charged with atmosphere. Arrivals and departures are always uppermost in mind, and the large clock in each terminal ticks out its daily schedule for the passengers who come and go in the day and the night. Happiness and sorrow mingle side by side as families, couples, or individuals occupy the terminal for brief periods of time. Life moves slowly and deliberately on, and nowhere is it more evident than at terminals of transportation.

Train yards and terminals are fascinating because of the noise and smell and because of life in constant motion.

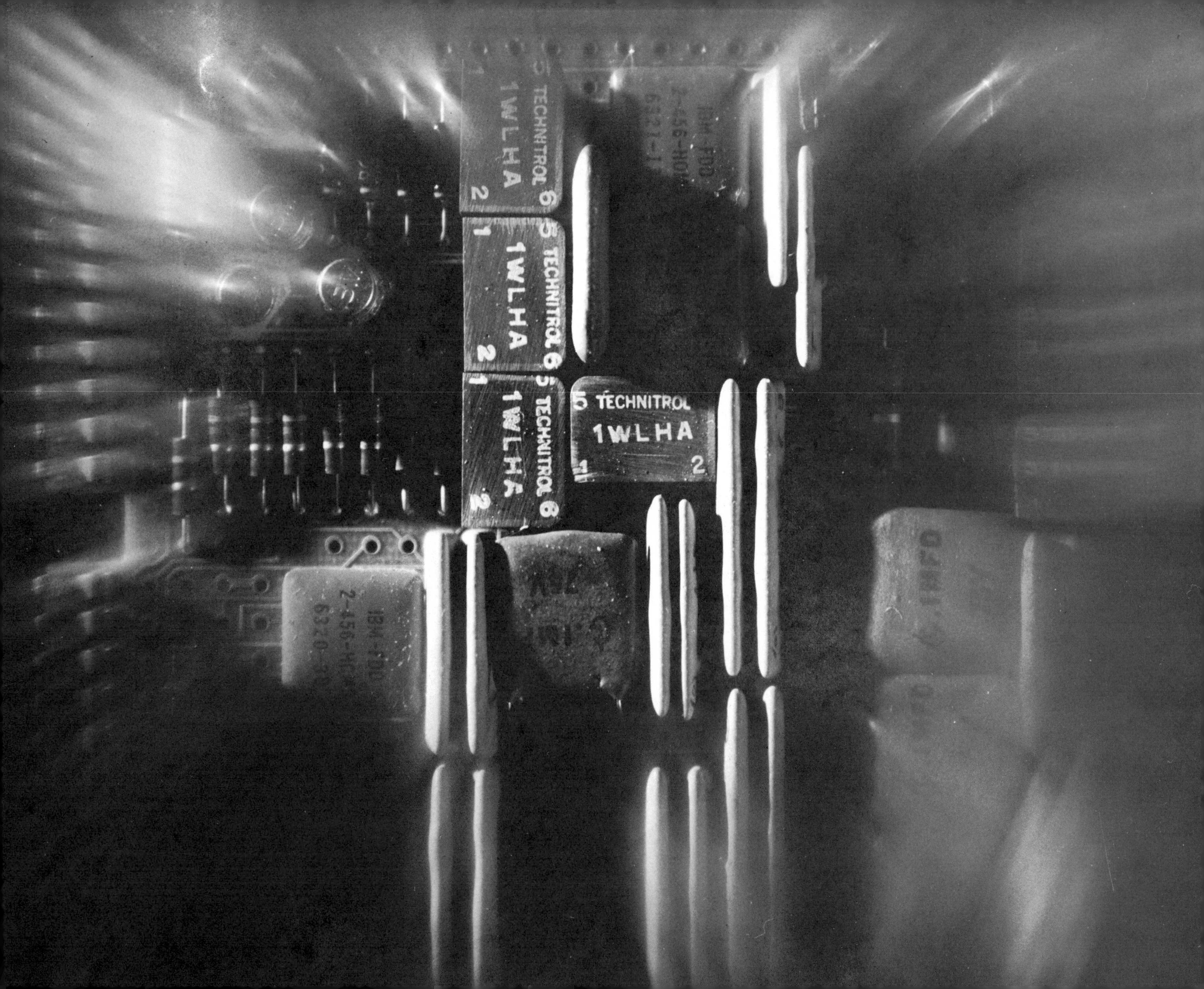
TECHNITROL
1WLHA

The artist is first and foremost a sensitive organism receiving visual and emotional stimuli from the outside world. These stimuli are absorbed and translated into the language of art through various technical media as well as through the artistic idiom of the time, rendered in the artist's personal manner.[1]

Chapter 4

Precision Instruments
Are Good Idea-Sparkers

A new world of aesthetic discovery opens when we investigate the realm of precision instruments. Within this specialized environment the beauty of motion is both visible and central to the processes involved. In a mechanical world of clocks and watches, relay systems, computers and signal systems of infinite variety, we can discover a continuous network of visual challenge.

One cannot predict exactly what elements or parts of a specific subject will open the trap to our imagination. An artist must develop an awareness for his subject first. It might take one, two, or a succession of visits to the site before an idea strikes. Often there has to be a period of expectancy before possible directions are suggested. Ideas need time to simmer and warm up. The interval between initial contact with a subject and the discovery of a solid aesthetic possibility may be days, months, or even years. Ideas for art come when

[1]Bernard S. Myers, from *Understanding the Arts,* Revised Edition. New York: Holt, Rinehart and Winston, Inc., 1963, p. 9.

77

we search for details that we might ordinarily overlook. Searching beneath the surface can reveal fascinating parts. Precision instruments offer such revelations: the protective shell must be removed in order to reach much of the visual beauty of the mechanism. There is nothing to match the suspense one feels when viewing for the first time the internal workings of a clock or a computer.

Tower Clocks Have Idea Potential

Tower clocks are not only mammoth, they are also difficult to reach. They can, however, be found in most towns. Some likely locations include a college campus, a train station, a courthouse and a town hall.

Tower clocks are impressive from the standpoint of sheer size. When we consider that most clocks can be held in the hand, the unusual size of the larger clock might serve as an aesthetic cue. Climbing into the tower or attic portion of a large public clock of this sort could be exciting indeed. Imagine being close to hands on a clock that are comparable to large iron bars and capable of holding the weight of several individuals. Many of these clocks possess bells or chimes that strike at periodic intervals. The view from the ground of one of these clocks should be considered for idea potential, as well as the eye level view from an adjoining building.

Grandfather Clocks Are Visual Delights

Tall clocks, nicknamed grandfather clocks, offer possibilities to the artist in the way of visual form. Both external and internal characteristics are worthy of study. The earlier tall clocks which are now of antique standing illustrate a particular charm.

Many of these clocks have embellishments inscribed or painted on the face. Commonly used decorative touches include the phases of the moon and designed touches of leaf and scroll patterns. The overall construction is of wood and metal with the pendulums hung inside the wood shell. They offer a pleasing metallic accent to the otherwise soft effect of the wood. The surface area immediately bordering the face on many tall clocks is often exquisitely modeled and carved to form a delicate lace work of artistic beauty. This detail provides an interesting contrast to the simplicity of the supporting elements of these clocks. The vertical thrust of tall clocks, coupled with the angular corners at both top and bottom, and the box-like shaft which connects the middle section suggest many directions for working in an art medium. These clocks would make wonderful subjects for ink drawing as well as painting. Another interesting feature of the tall clock from the standpoint of the aesthetic eye, is the construction of the casing at the top of the clock. Columns elaborately carved in the Greek vein are often included, as well as various pinnacles and knobs of the craftsman's hand. All in all, these slender giants offer much to the artist in the way of unusual subject matter.

Banjo, Coffin and Other Stylish Wall Clocks

The notion of time as an aesthetic consideration can be fascinating. Georgio de Chirico, the surrealist painter was intrigued by physical time and treated it poetically in his paintings. It has also been interpreted in an individual manner by Salvador Dali, another surrealist painter. The clock as a symbolic consideration represents the passing of all things. It stands as a concrete reminder that nothing is forever, yet forever is in everything.

An extensive variety of clock
types awaits the searcher in
this realm: the forms are
exquisite to behold.

Courtesy, Pioneer Museum and Haggin Galleries,
Stockton, California

Courtesy, Dorothy and Ralph Langwick

Jon Geil

Reproduced from Moire Kit #70,719,
by permission of Edmund Scientific Co.,
101 E. Gloucester Pike, Barrington, New Jersey

"Homage to the Square: Silent Hall," (1961), Josef Albers
Oil on composition board, 40 x 40".
Collection, The Museum of Modern Art, New York
Dr. and Mrs. Frank Stanton Fund.

The passage of time might
be represented in visual terms.
Scientific patterns as well as
experimental art works which
emphasize optical effects and
space could suggest possibilities in this direction.

There is interesting visual material in clocks that were designed to hang on walls. Wall clocks are probably the more diversified of the timepieces; styles include the coffin type, banjo type, lyre type, and several others. These styles are imitated today and can be found in most department stores. The antique variety may offer more appeal in terms of surface patina and weathering. The ornateness of many of these clocks would be especially suitable for a decorative interpretation with art media. Some clocks are covered with glittering statuary and gilded shells. Cupids and cherubs abound, perpetually frolicking among the leaves and other ornamental whimseys of the clockmaker. Many clocks of this variety have miniature paintings on the face, and on the front cabinet at the base. Many of these clocks would seem ideal as subject matter for the collage or montage type of construction.

Clocks are such a characteristic part of our society that the passing of time as an ideational motive might be examined in several ways. Sun dials, one of the original time indicators, could indicate several directions for further exploration. A winding mechanism for the clock, such as the key, presents a stimulating possibility for the artistic mind. Ordinary keys do not jar the idea sense, but let the imagination travel to the old jailer keys — the keys that were used to lock the castle, or the dungeons. One has visions of leg irons, chains, and huge, rusty keys that attach to a single iron band at the waist. A key of this type could be adapted to an equally fancy treatment of an ornate clock and a fresh series of ideas is underway. Yes, the keys that wind clocks could be fancy indeed. Remember, we are contemplating possibilities. The imagination must be stoked if aesthetic fires are to burn. Once we have experienced the subject under view and we are completely familiar with the characteristics therein, it is time to give the imagination full throttle. There can be no inhibiting at the beginning of discovery. One must give himself fully to the ideas which may come to mind.

Becoming an artist means learning to see with both vision *and* intellect. We do not see with the eyes alone. They merely give us our jumping-off point to aesthetic adventure. The real job of creation lies at the depth of our being, and every niche and cranny must be jarred if the fullest expression is to flow forth. Art is never made by individuals who skim the surface of life.

Gears and Pendulums

Another exciting realm in the study of clocks and watches pertains to their internal functions. Once the backing is removed, a gleaming wealth of springs, coils, release mechanisms, power trains, and armatures is revealed to the searching eye. The insides of clocks are like tiny factories which contain all the necessary parts to do the proper job. On an even smaller scale, watches contain a world in miniature that is unmatched for unified parts in motion. When viewing the inside portions of a watch one is reminded of the fanciful art works of the Swiss artist Paul Klee.

Electronic Computers and Their Brains

Computers have been referred to as thinking machines, or electronic brains. They are programed to play games, compose musical verse, calculate extremely complex formulas, control missiles in space, and carry out infinitely extensive operations. Computers are by far one of man's highest achievements within the inventive boundaries of society. If we step beyond the functional capacity of these instruments, the sheer beauty of the detailed parts can hold visual magic for the artist. Even the wires are colored to provide aesthetic emphasis. While the artist does not see the operational sequences of such machines with the same understanding as the technician, such processes can hold source material for artistic production. The artist shares

Studying the details of electronic equipment and other types of machinery enables one to focus on specific parts relative to aesthetic considerations. Personal awareness is increased when we move beyond surface generalizations.

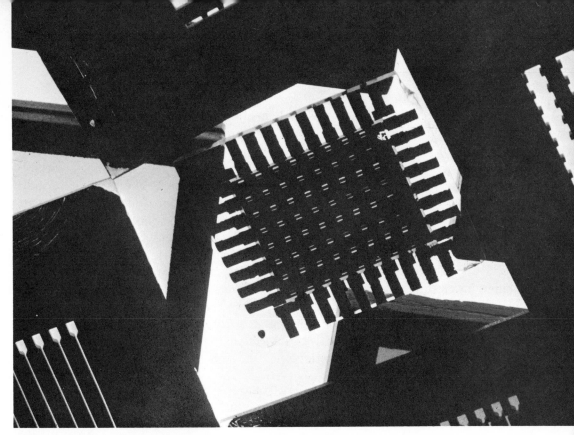

Courtesy, International Business Machines Corporation, White Plains, New York

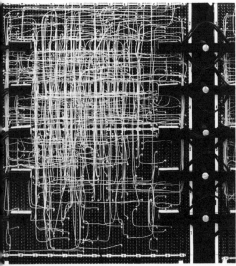

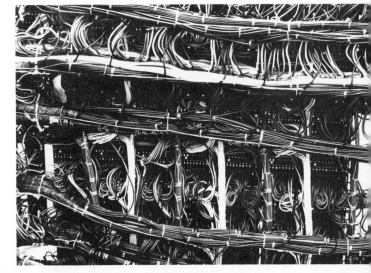

Courtesy, International Business Machines Corporation, White Plains, New York

Courtesy, International Business Machines Corporation, White Plains, New York

Ralph Talbert

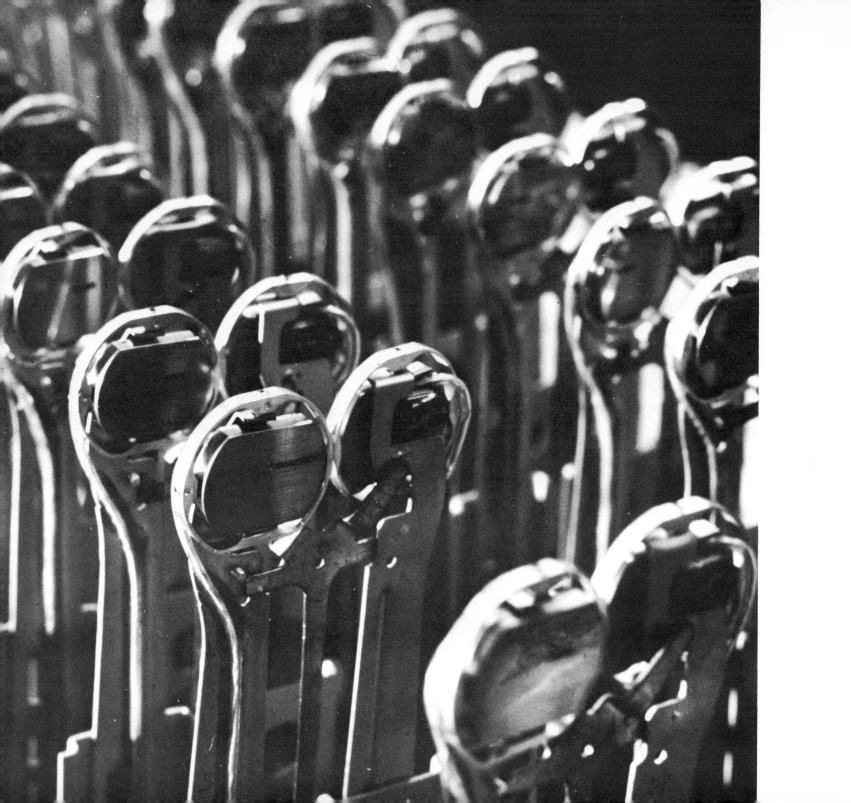

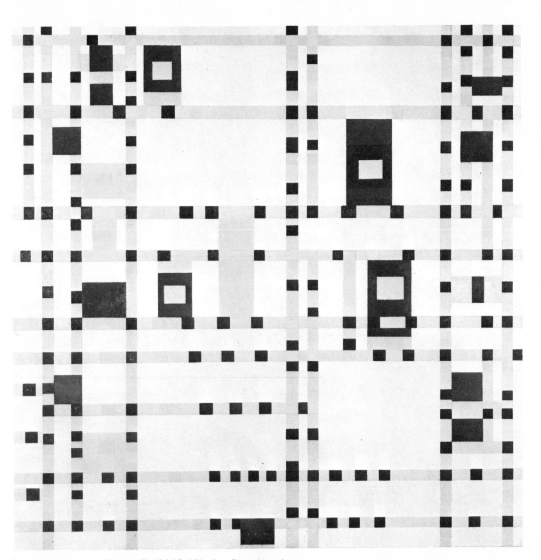

"Broadway Boogie Woogie" (1942-43), by Piet Mondrian
Oil on canvas, 50 x 50"
Collection, The Museum of Modern Art, New York

The rhythm and the motion of the
machine offer complex visual stimuli
to the searching eye.

"Suprematist Composition: White on White" (1918?), by Kasimir Malevich
Oil on canvas 31¼ x 31¼"
Courtesy, The Museum of Modern Art, New York

Qualities of aesthetic form are often subtle in both utilitarian form and artistic product. Quiet rhythms move slowly in and through the visual atmosphere of the subject.

in the wonder that science has wrought, but his purpose is as a seeker of beauty — a huntsman of aesthetic form. Electronic computers are visual targets of the highest order. They are a vast network of tubes, wires, signal systems, patterned circuits, and colored units. Much of the beauty of their form lies in a combination of speed, precision, and contemporary construction.

Tubes can be observed in row after row. They are of various sizes according to their specific electrical function within an ever-changing pattern of beautiful sequences. Such sequences are evidenced by the soft glow of the tubes as information is fed into the machines by magnetic tapes. One can discover an infinite variety of patterns and repetitive harmonies that often resemble a woven fabric, so closely are the wires and tubings interconnected. The lighting systems, and the movements that are observable by the transmission of electrical impulses suggest possibilities for abstract compositions. The artist must ask himself how the visually perceived motion of the electrical circuits can be interpreted with pigment or other art media. Being able to produce original ideas, or to see the potential of a subject is one of the earmarks of the inventive artistic personality. The artist often does more than imitate what he sees. He takes definite steps that lead him far beyond the mere illustration of the subject.

The computers' memory banks, which store particles of information, are highly interesting as dynamic visual phenomena. Viewing the insides of a computer is analogous to seeing thousands of bees in a hive. There is almost too much for the eye to take in at one observation.

Other Instruments and Their Parts

The excitement of precision can be discovered in most automatic machines that are presently produced. One has only to remove the outer covering in order to see pleasing forms. The artist or student could begin his search by removing the outer casing from any type of machine, i. e., a typewriter, calculator, or telephone. It would be profitable to go straight to a factory where such items as radios, television sets, automobile engines, or other instruments and machines are constructed. Artists such as Charles Sheeler, Fernand Léger, Stuart Davis, and I. Rice Pereira have explored and discovered the artistic potential in such machines. Consulting the works of artists such as these who have undertaken similar aesthetic challenges with machines and instruments would be helpful in suggesting possible directions to follow.

Industrial piping and other connecting structures are good subject material because of the robot-like characteristics which are suggested by the maze of interconnections. Although subject material of this variety is enormous in physical scale, precision instruments can range in size from ultra-miniature circuits, watches and surgical motors, to jet engines and telescopes for probing outer space.

Printed circuits for electrical connections of television sets and other electronic apparatus can be fascinating as idea potential. They resemble calligraphic impressions randomly organized and fused to a stamped form. While the printed circuit has helped to shrink the size of radio and television sets, the combination of such miniature parts has created a wonderful source of interesting forms. An artist could sit for hours and draw the combined parts without running out of ideas. Colored inks with black would make an excellent sketching medium for this type of subject. Rice paper and other absorbent papers would be suitable for obtaining some unusual effects.

The material that is fed into many electronic machines should not be overlooked. Punched cards and tape, and other forms of paper tape might lead to intriguing directions. There are several pathways that one might explore with the paper tape and punched cards. They could serve as a source of collage material. Another approach would be to enlarge the actual appearance of a segment of the tape and transfer it to the canvas or drawing surface. The punched holes would provide a means to place colors and tonal qualities in a controlled rhythm. The tape could serve as a variation on the approach developed by Piet Mondrian with his now famous squares and rectangles. Those interested in the optical effects of color might see avenues for experimentation here.

Another source possibility for art could relate to the mathematical and figurative material that is fed into the various machines. Imagine cosines, equations, and square roots redefined into a compositional arrangement! Most visual diagrams of this nature have eye appeal apart from their function. There is a certain artistic beauty in viewing a complicated mathematical relationship. Stuart Davis has successfully utilized symbols and other abbreviated signs within his paintings. Binary digits, word fragments, musical notes, and various numbering systems can be united with color, composition, and personal technique to create original statements in paint. Mathematical texts and scientific journals are appropriate sources for obtaining such formulas and related material.

Many of the individual parts of computers, radios, and other electrically powered instruments are worthy of investigation. Resistors, tubes, capacitors, inductors, component leads and other miniature electrical parts remind one of the appendage networks of spiders and insects. There is some visual similarity between viewing a box full of tiny electrodes and a sac full of baby spiders. One of the attributes of a mature artist is his ability to see the relationship of forms. He is able to put opposites together to form the whole. This is done at all stages of the artistic process. Something observed in nature may form the basis for a non-objective abstraction on canvas. There need be no obvious relationship of idea and material.

Old typewriters have a marvelous sculptural quality that could serve as subject potential. There are many gadget parts within these clacking forms. The keys are attached to slender appendages that dart underneath a protective plating and disappear into the middle of the machine. The variety of forms in a typewriter is especially suitable for drawing or other detailed work in art. Searching for outdated models of various machines can be rewarding. Remember the wonderful forms of the old-time cars? There is a look of individualism about these early cars. They have the same "feel" as the styling of the early typewriters. There is a hand-crafted appearance that suggests a certain individuality of design. All too often today, automobiles, sewing machines, typewriters, and tape dispensers have the same look of "speed"; the jet look. Sometimes we have to search in depth. Taking an old machine apart could reveal strange forms to excite the aesthetic eye.

Packaging machines would be highly suitable sources for idea discoveries. Such machines bottle or package every conceivable product from eggs, soft drinks and milk, to sandwiches, frozen foods, candy and canned goods. Many of these machines have a series of related actions that must be performed before the process can be repeated. Precise timing is necessary for the entire operational procedure. The presence of so many parts and gears would be stimulating for the artist to view. The artist could go directly to the bakery, or the manufacturing plant and witness the machines in action.

Radar scopes, screens, blip signals, and sonic devices should be included within this category of precision instruments. Anything of this nature which offers a visual diagram in the form

"Seven-up" by Robert Arneson
Courtesy of the artist

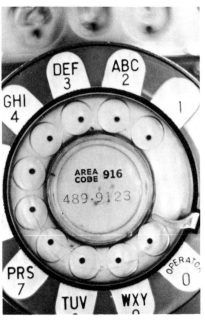

It is difficult to know exactly what subject will spark the urge to create. Each person must find his world in his own way.

"Lidded Stoneware Jar"
by Carl B. Cassady
Courtesy, Crocker Art Gallery,
Sacramento, California

The artist, Ed Larson,
at work on "Man and His Machines"
Courtesy, San Juan Unified School District,
Sacramento, California

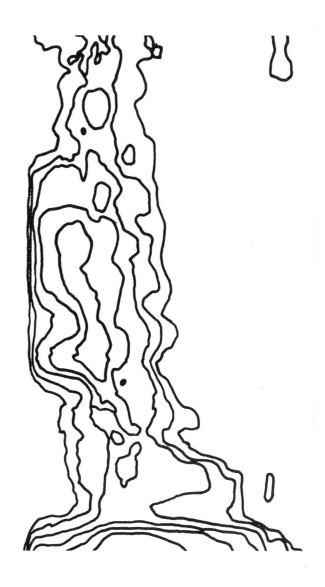

The human voice has been recorded and interpreted in visual form as seen in the two examples above. Control of the visual path is determined by intensity, pitch, and frequency. The relation here between linear form and other aesthetic cues suggests pertinent directions for further exploration.

Courtesy, Crocker Art Gallery,
Sacramento, California

"Three Women," (Le grand dejeuner), 1921, by Fernand Leger
Oil on canvas, 72¼ x 99"
Collection, The Museum of Modern Art, New York.
Mrs. Simon Guggenheim Fund.

In certain instances the forms
of the subject are echoed in
the material the artist uses.
The precision of the machine
has its counterpart in the expressive forms of both painter
and craftsman.

of lighting systems, tracking devices, and electrical impulse signals can serve as a visual cue for the artist.

This is the age of the chrome-spun metallic finish with a super-high-par polish. The precision of the machine is as American as the hot dog. It is only natural that the artist should search through the maze of utilitarian forms and attempt to establish some aesthetic rapport with this breed of product. For those who seek new challenges of artistic ideas, these hunting grounds offer a considerable basis for exploration.

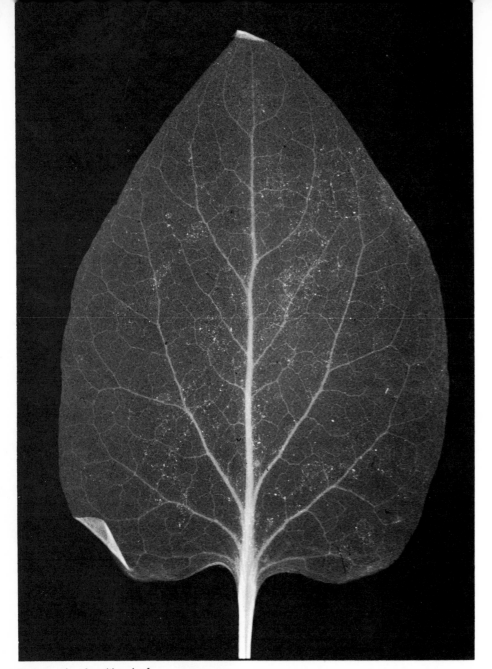

Radiograph of a lilac leaf,
Courtesy, Eastman Kodak Company

"The narrow bud opens her beauties to
The sun, and love runs in her thrilling veins;
Blossoms hang round the brows of morning, and
Flourish down the bright cheek of modest eve,
Till clust'ring Summer breaks forth into singing,
And feather'd clouds strew flowers round her head."[1]

Chapter 5

An Artistic View
of Flowers and Growing Things

The curving shape of a leaf, the twist of a tree limb, the gentle grace of a blossom in bloom; all reflect an unharnessed beauty within natural forms which offers the art student a continual source of aesthetic stimulation. The aspiring artist must become aware of these details within the larger, more haphazard landscape. More intense searching can reveal the underlying structure of seed and petal growth, the textural quality of a stem, or the subtle changes in light values from petal to petal as sunlight skips across surfaces. By extending our awareness, we can discover how a tree anchors itself to the soil, why a daisy grows in clusters, and how a mass of granite pushes upward in a silent crescendo. Experimentations of this type, coupled with a keen edge for discovery are the fuel which charges one's artistic appetite!

---

[1]"To Autumn" by William Blake.

Seeing in Depth

Discovering ideas in nature presents some difficulty because we must learn to separate the vast general milieu of information which comes to our eyes and select those aspects which will be useful in an artistic sense. To do this, we must study natural forms in all of their magnitude and then interpret in an individual manner. Each artist must see the landscape in his own way and utilize the forms that are most significant for him. This indicates that he must examine trees, flowers, stems, plants, ferns, moss, and all that grows in both forest and field. Much of what one experiences at the moment will not be immediately applicable to an art work. Instead, this information becomes a backlog and a reservoir of impressions for later paintings.

Although nature is a product of natural order, man cannot follow it exactly in organizing his painting. He must take the coarse, natural subject and organize it into cohesive relationships. The artist could begin his search for idea material at any point, anywhere; by examining flowers or trees or some other natural form at hand. Reading books on the subject could broaden the aesthetic viewpoint. Observation alone may not be sufficient for some artists. Learning the technical aspects, such as the terminology of plants and other biological data may enhance one's visual understanding. Nature is a vast, impressive arena and if the artist is to gain artistic toe holds he must develop a broad grasp of his subject. Knowledge of a subject strengthens the artistic statement for it permits the artist a wider range of expression.

Sources for Discovery

The source material which can be discovered in natural forms is literally inexhaustable. The boundaries of one's immediate surroundings can serve as a beginning location. It is not necessary to travel to the north pole, or the equator to gain the proper stimulus for art. The richness of natural growth can be studied in a garden, a field, or on a nearby hillside. It can be found in greenhouses, nurseries, and flower shops.

Each student must search in the locations that strike responsive chords. Where one person will see possibilities for decorative experimentation, another will see pure abstraction. Still another will desire to express the subject in a manner that closely matches what exists. It should be stated that the purposes of having experiences with natural forms and with the other subjects which are suggested in these chapters is to *keep individual curiosity at its highest point*. It must always be kept *in mind* that art works cannot be created by the *vacant mind*.

A solid approach in studying natural form might be to take a specific object such as a flower or a weed pod which has been dried, and dissect it piece by piece to learn the various parts. The next step might consist of drawing each piece accurately, or seeing how many ways the same part can be interpreted. Here again, temperament and other personal factors would enter in to influence the approach. One artist will lean toward the external appearance of the flower; more than likely, this could indicate a landscape painter. Another artist might draw his source material from what he sees on the inside of the flower and this could suggest a more abstract style. There are no demarcation lines for art. There *are* ways of working with an art medium and subject. The more ways that a student of art can practice, the greater will be his chances for success. Know-how-man-ship in art comes when the artist is willing to put plenty of zest into the process. It should be added at this point that ideas for art flow readily when there is an ample supply of digested information concerning the subject. Each artist has to decide which aspects in nature will be his springboards for ideas. The fluent, innovating person is one who can give us the

Observation of the subject may not be enough to capture what is there. Investigating in depth with the aid of special equipment enables us to see inside as well as outside and thus form a more comprehensive image.

Radiograph of an orchid,
Courtesy, Eastman Kodak Company

"Flowers and Sea" by Don Reich
Courtesy, Crocker Art Gallery,
Sacramento, California

Each part of the flower or plant should be examined; every bit of information will strengthen the final artistic statement. One must know his subject well if he is to express ideas in an imaginative vein.

Jon Geil

fresh view, the unusual twist. He is the Picasso or the Wyeth. However, every artist or artist-to-be who is worth his mettle will learn to say his ideas uniquely.

In studying the characteristics of flowers, the artist might find it helpful to investigate the biological characteristics of the plant. One can also perceive several variations from flower to flower. Some are rounded, some drooping, some pointed, some stiff in appearance. Some contain a hard, exterior covering. Others are prickly. All flowers possess subtle graces of color and scent. Even so, some flowers appear dangerous, having thorny barbs or other protective coatings. Many flowers of the cactus family are of this variety. Some flowers are extremely delicate and soft, such as the rose or the lily. Smaller flowers have a gentleness that is appealing to the aesthetic sense.

Further examination of flowers can reveal many details that would go unnoticed at a glance. Some items to check for include dew on the petals, nectar, stamens, pistils, and stalks. The cycle of a flower from bud stage to seed would give interesting source ideas. Flowers seen under varying conditions can change one's responses. Cut flowers, for example, evoke a different feeling from flowers that we see growing in a field. Flowers in a sick room emit an odor that is different from the same type of flowers used as decoration at a wedding.

Some idea possibilities in composing pictures with flowers as a subject, might include an arrangement of flowers that are of different varieties but identical in terms of color. For instance, how would an artist handle a bouquet of white flowers arranged against a background of white? It might be interesting to arrange a group of miniature flowers, such as forget-me-nots, sweet peas, and violets. We might arrange flowers all of one variety, such as roses. The variations are as extensive as there are artists to invent such arrangements. It might be challenging

to paint both inside and outside views in the same composition. Diagrams of plant cross-sections which reveal minute details could serve as stimulating idea material. It is always profitable to study books that show diagrams of cytoplasm, nuclei, and other structures of the flower.

An interesting aspect to consider in observing flowers is to notice the variations in the positioning of the petals. Each point of view of the observer can offer much in terms of tonal articulation and depth of field. As light strikes on surfaces, the petals take on various shades of tone. The texture of flowers will affect the visual appearance also. Some flowers are extremely fuzzy, while others are shiny smooth. Flowers that contain a profuse amount of thistles, points, spurs, and other barbs create lovely shadow patterns. The effect of shadows, the manner in which one petal falls across another can result in a fascinating interplay of light. Some flowers open out in the morning hours while others blossom at nightfall so that light patterns are continually shifting. An interesting possibility might deal with drawing flowers at dusk, or under a failing light. A foggy or misty atmosphere would be a nice setting for a composition of flowers.

Sometimes flowers can be studied under conditions of unusual light. That is, the flowers may appear as a blue, violet, green, or grayish blur depending on the colors involved in the scene. For example, when flowers are seen in the rain they have a completely different character. Actually, the variations under which flowers can be observed are almost limitless. The number of sources is controlled only by our own limitations in this respect. One individual will appear to have an unlimited depth of imaginative ideas from a subject, while another individual may indicate difficulty in *any* type of serious contact with the same subject. *Creative depth of thinking requires constant practice in stretching the boundaries of our imagination and intellect.*

"Gold and Violet Still Life"
by Claude Venard
Courtesy, Crocker Art Gallery,
Sacramento, California

Courtesy, Crocker Art Gallery,
Sacramento, California

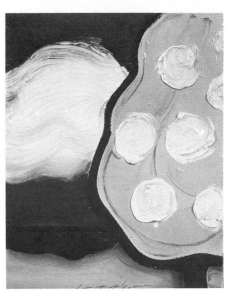

"Tree" by Ken Waterstreet
Courtesy of the artist

Wild flowers are somewhat different in character from the ordinary cultivated varieties that we are accustomed to. They are somewhat scrubbier and rougher as a lot. They possess an intangible sensitivity that speaks of earthiness; a bridge with untouched natural forms. They are smaller, scarcer, and are found in the most unusual places; between crevices, on steep hillsides, in quiet forest glens, and other less accessible sources. Wild flowers are also found along highways and in fields, but more often than not they are part of the countryside that is equally exciting to discover.

Another interesting aspect to consider in studying flowers deals with size. Some flowers in various parts of the world reach tremendous proportions. Of particular mention in this respect are some flowers which grow in Sumatra, a portion of the island group that forms part of the Dutch East Indies. In these islands, flowers attain petal lengths in excess of one foot per petal. Other plants which have gigantic flowers also have weights exceeding 100 pounds. Another flower which grows on the top of the Amazon river in South America is the Royal Water Lily. This plant has leaves which reach a diameter of five to six feet. This seems incredible if we think in terms of ordinary flower and plant sizes. This fact alone could open the door to many imaginative adventures with interpretations of flowers. How would a flower of such size be presented on canvas? In what other media could it be explored?

Ideas From Desert Growth

The most significant plants that grow on the desert include the strange but beautiful types known as cactus. Cactuses are of many different varieties and descriptions. Many of them are thorny, prickly, and have a character of their own. From an artistic viewpoint it is exciting to deal with such angular, barbed forms in contrast to the soft, delicate forms of cultivated flowers.

Desert growth has sensitivity of form also, but it is particularly noted for its armor plating. Such exterior covering makes creation with aesthetic media appealing. Most shapes of cactus are unusual. They are somewhat oddball in character, due to their need for survival under unusual climatic conditions. Cactus plants usually consist of soft greens and muted tones of gray and tan. They reach astounding heights. Twenty feet is a not uncommon height in the cactus family. The barbs, thorns, and spearheads of the cactus plants twist and turn in a variety of directions and upward thrusts that are well suited for artistic arrangements. The diagonal thrusts of the thorny barbs are well suited for interpretation by short, jabbing strokes of the brush. The overall movement of the cactus as an aesthetic form is one of verticality.

Trees Inspire Art Forms

There are untold gems waiting for the art student when he directs his idea search to trees: the following discussion is intended to serve as a beginning direction for anyone interested in exploring further in this area. One impressive species of tree includes the giant Sequoia, probably the largest tree in existence in the world today. Sequoias are the oldest and most massive of trees, and actually form a link with our prehistoric past. Some of these big fellows were in existence more than 2,000 years ago, and are very much alive today! The trunk diameters have been measured at 21 feet. Imagine standing next to a giant of this order. The furrows in the bark are so large, they resemble fissures made by trucks on muddy roads in winter. These kings of the forest have a stately appearance, a tremendous muscular feel. When one enters near Sequoias, the emotional impact is immediate. Trees of this size remind us of fairy tale stories of childhood. One imagines Robin Hood, the Three Bears, and Hanzel and Gretel behind each trunk. While observing these stately masters, one could surely be moved to create such a scene in pigment.

While much in nature is gentle and delicate to the touch and eye, some forms are irregular in shape with coats of thorny, protective armor.

Ralph Talbert

Ralph Talbert

The forest is an inspiring location for the artist to be. There are all manners and varieties of trees. In many sections of the forest, the sun has difficulty breaking through because of the density of the foliage. When light does filter down, it is like the light in a cathedral. The most likely approach for the artist in examining trees in both forest and field is to search for pleasing relationships of whatever the eye can take in. Trees are beautiful wherever they are found. In an older tree, there is gnarling and many of the branches sag with the weight of years. All branches dip when rain or snow is heavy. There are many possibilities to consider when studying trees as subject potential. Some factors to study include: trees in winter with or without leaves, trees in summer and fall, trees with rain and snow on the branches, trees in clusters, trees alone, sturdy old trees, thin, wispy saplings, and so forth.

Some trees are slender and have a delicate appearance such as the gray birch, which has a grayish bark with a broken sequence of patches extending along the trunk. These trees have exquisite coloring of the leaves in the fall — a factor to consider in watercolor painting.

The mighty oaks grow in most parts of the United States. This type of tree is massive and appealing to view. The branches are often of a curling, pendulous nature, and hang nearly to the ground. The oak trees are the ones that often hold the rope and improvised tire swing. Oaks are of many varieties including northern and southern oaks, and laurel oak. The laurel oak is an interesting tree. It grows mainly in Florida, Georgia and Louisiana. It has huge branches that lift upward to the sky. Other trees to investigate include the dogwood, the sycamore, the magnolia with its beautiful flowers, and the firs and redwoods. The firs and pines grow very straight and tall and display a beautiful coat of needles and cones.

Some other characteristics to consider in the search for aesthetic ideas include the light and dark patterns caused by sunlight, root systems of trees that grow near and around marshes or in tropical sections of the world, and trees that are continually buffeted by the wind and ocean mist. Trees with extensive root systems include the mangrove in Malayan swamps, where roots interlace with mud and marsh to form an almost impenetrable thicket. Wind-swept trees which cling to survival can be found along the ocean coasts. A fine example of this type is the Monterey Cypress which is found along the coast near Monterey, California. Other wind-swept firs and pines can be studied along the length of any coastline.

The artistic searcher can find idea material from the exploration of palm trees. While these trees are found only in the warmer regions of the world, one should not restrict his eye to local subjects. Books, films, and illustrations can help us to build ideas from subjects that cannot be reached. One interesting aspect of the palm tree is its leaf structure. The leaves are large, pointed, and have an appealing needle point series of edges. Palm trees stand very tall, with some varieties reaching heights of 200 feet and more. The trunk is a vertical shaft that contains overlapping portions of bark, thus providing the palm with a pleasing textural surface. We tend to associate the palm with jungles and tropical regions of the world where monkeys and coconuts abound. For many purposes, the palm is exotic as a plant form and would lend itself well to detailed interpretation with art media.

Insectivorous Plants as Idea Sources

It might be an intriguing experience to consider as idea potential plants which consume insects and other forms of animal matter in order to obtain the nutrients for growth. Plants of this

The surface characteristics of tree forms vary from tree to tree. The ends and root systems offer unusual visual information.

East African Tree
Courtesy, Edward S. Ross, Curator, California Academy of Sciences

Lino on fabric by Mary J. Rouse
Courtesy of the artist

Early Oriental artist
Courtesy, Crocker Art Gallery,
Sacramento, California

"Delta, P.M." by David Dangelo
Courtesy of the artist

Painting by Pieter Breughel
Courtesy, Crocker Art Gallery,
Sacramento, California

While the subject or content may
be taken from a similar source,
interpretation always remains individual and personal. The art
work is an interpretation of the
artist's vision from the stimulus.

"Olive Harvest" by Monica Hannasch
Courtesy, Crocker Art Gallery,
Sacramento, California

The sensitive observer takes in an extensive variety of information relating to a specific subject. A rich idea-bank forms the basis for strong personal statements in art media.

nature capture insects alive, immobolize them, and absorb their juices. Some plants of this variety that would be fascinating to explore for ideas include the pitcher plant, Venus's flytrap, and the sun dew. These plants are magnificent in both color and external design. The pitcher plant captures its prey because of the slickness of its surface: insects crawl on the inside leaf walls and slip to the bottom when a certain point is reached; or they scamper to the bottom of the leaf wall to drink the liquid and find that the walls are too steep and slippery to get out. They eventually drown and are absorbed by the plant.

In the case of Venus's flytrap, it has leaves that clamp shut much like a vice or jaw. When insects crawl across the leaf, tiny trigger hairs spring the trap and the top leaf closes in a split second to meet the bottom leaf, thus capturing the insect. The plant operates much in the manner of an alligator. Whatever goes in doesn't come out.

The sun dew is an extremely beautiful plant which glistens with color and nectar. This plant operates in a manner similar to an octopus. It has a series of tentacles that remain open until some foreign particle such as an insect lands on one. The sticky liquid of the plant holds the insect while the thorny exterior surface pulls it down into the heart of the plant.

Plants of this nature are found growing in bogs and marshes in some sections of the United States. Actually, they are not large in size, yet their functions and methods of acquiring food are exotic. It would appear that many directions for art ideas could be uncovered by exploring sources such as these.

The Beauty of Ferns and Fungus

An interesting group which is found in many sections of the United States, particularly in areas of extensive rainfall, is the family of ferns. Their numbers are extensive, and the variety is almost limitless. They are lovely, non-flowering green-leaved plants which thrive in shaded woodlands and forest groves. Ferns have an appeal that is suggestive of Pacific island paradises. Ferns are interesting from the aesthetic point of view because they are delicate, lacy in appearance and cover the ground with a green, green blanket. The repetitious structural character of the plant is appropriately suited to design experimentation in art media.

The searcher of the beautiful form will be delighted to discover another area which is a continual source of stimulation. We are referring to the family of fungus: the toadstool, mushroom, and others of this variety. Some fungi take the form of the substance that they are growing from. Other types grow from a central shaft that comes up from the ground, from wood, or from a source of decay. The higher forms of fungi are known as mushrooms and toadstools while the lower forms are referred to as molds. These types of plant forms keep both forest and earth free of decay and rot. They are the scavengers of life, and help to maintain the balance in nature by living off the dead matter of plants, insects, leaves, and other organic matter.

One interesting feature of mushrooms is that they grow in a repetitive manner. The shapes are numerous and include cylindrical, kidney and heart forms, and pointed bell types. Some fungi are almost shell-like and are reminiscent of marine forms. Actually, the forms of fungus are so numerous that an artist would have an extensive selection should he decide to explore shape and structure. At the lower end of the fungus group are the molds. They consist of soft, gelatinous material or other substances that are dampish in character. Molds are also characterized by a fuzzy surface texture. The student working with ceramic clay might find some appealing directions in this type of subject material.

Jon Geil

Internal detail of an orange

Boyd Jensen

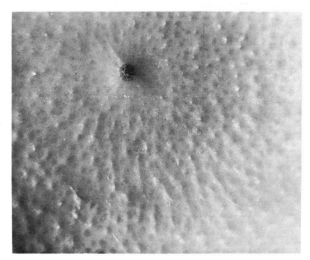

External detail of an orange

Boyd Jensen

Much of the beauty of fruit lies beneath the external covering. Slicing through fruit in various directions can reveal a wealth of aesthetic potential.

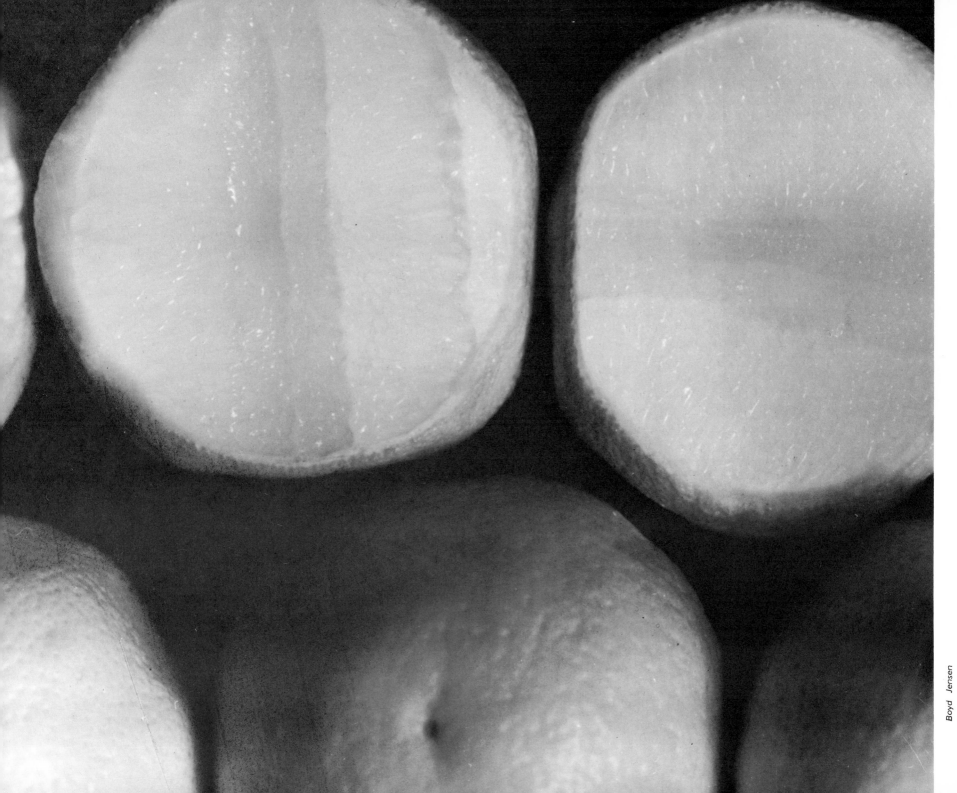

Vegetables and Fruit: Pure Beauty of Form

Vegetables and fruits offer the art student an excellent source for idea growth. Citrus fruits such as oranges, grapefruits, and lemons provide subtle variations of spherical structure. Fruit of this sort and related varieties can be studied as single items or in clusters. One good method of discovering the visual properties of a lemon, for example, is to study internal as well as external characteristics. This is done by slicing through the fruit. Many indications of design structure can be uncovered by the method in which the fruit is sliced. Slicing on the long axis exposes a different cell pattern than slicing in cross-section. There is more subject material available when internal sources are considered. Dealing *only* with the surface of a subject restricts artistic vision, for it shows us external characteristics without insight into structure.

When studying fruits in combination, one might make a still life arrangement and then search for compositional possibilities. Tonal properties, color relationships, and considerations of shape and texture are apparent directions for exploration. Some environmental situations which make suitable idea sources include the examination of fruit in a grocery bin, on a truck going to market, on the tree, and on the table. Interpretations in art media can range from conventional illustration to the more imaginative variations. Pastel provides a ready color source for experimentation on location. Graphic materials enable one to establish linear contact.

Most fruits are visually exciting when sliced in various manners. Pomegranates are particularly appealing because of the sizable number of seeds. The outer shell is unusual in appearance and makes an excellent subject for design experimentation. Apples are highly varied in terms of external shape and color, and offer the artist solid subject potential. Watermelons and cantalopes provide source ideas for consideration of shape as well as color.

Vegetables are somewhat more coarse in appearance and offer a splendid variety of textures, shapes, and colors. Squash in particular are interesting because of the extensive variations of each type. Most vegetables have leafy stalks and appendages that contribute to their eye appeal.

The way to get the most from fruits and vegetables is to collect a variety of them and arrange them in as many different positions as possible. The question to ask oneself here is: *how many ways can I discover to interpret the form?* When an artist has been able to interpret a subject in many ways, he is more fully equipped to make a selective judgment. Working directly in an art medium can lead the artist to discovery. The following statements could serve as a beginning approach with a subject such as fruits and vegetables:

Start by drawing the forms.
Draw the same form with ink, charcoal, pastel, pencils, and variations of brush and pen.
Change the true color of the form to its opposite hue, or an off-beat tone.
Build the form with paper and glues.
Use the paint in thickly prepared applications to achieve qualities of form.
Interpret the form under various conditions of light and shadow.
Abstract, exaggerate, and distort the form in as many ways as possible.
Experiment with a great variety of color variations.
Express the subject in a forceful manner, in a subtle manner, and with variations in between.
Work only with mass.
Work only with line.
Interpret the form as a transparency.
Wet the paper and work wet.
Incorporate glues, varnishes, and cements into the process.
Bring out the textural aspects and subdue other elements.

A listing of this sort could go on indefinitely depending on the fluency of the artist. There are hundreds of approaches in just one subject! Each subject undertaken should be considered in this manner. Selective choices of preferred art media can be better judged when one has a working knowledge of many types and varieties of material. The artist needs a *range* of understanding at the start, and a *depth* of approach when he is ready to explore vigorously.

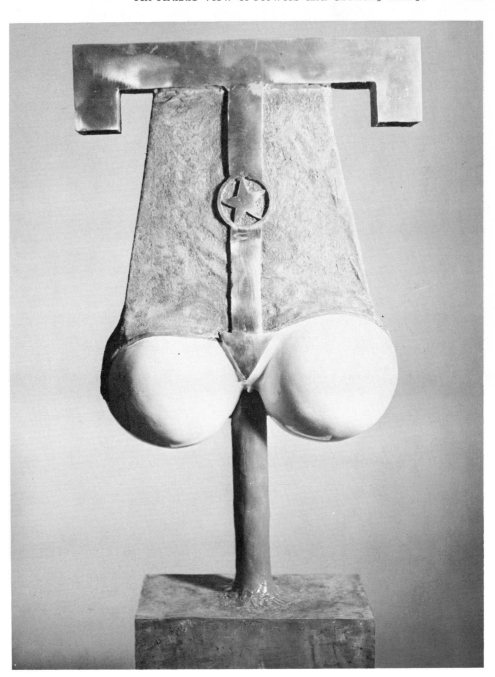

"Play-Tex" by Robert Arneson bronze casting and paint. Courtesy of Crocker Art Gallery, Sacramento, California.

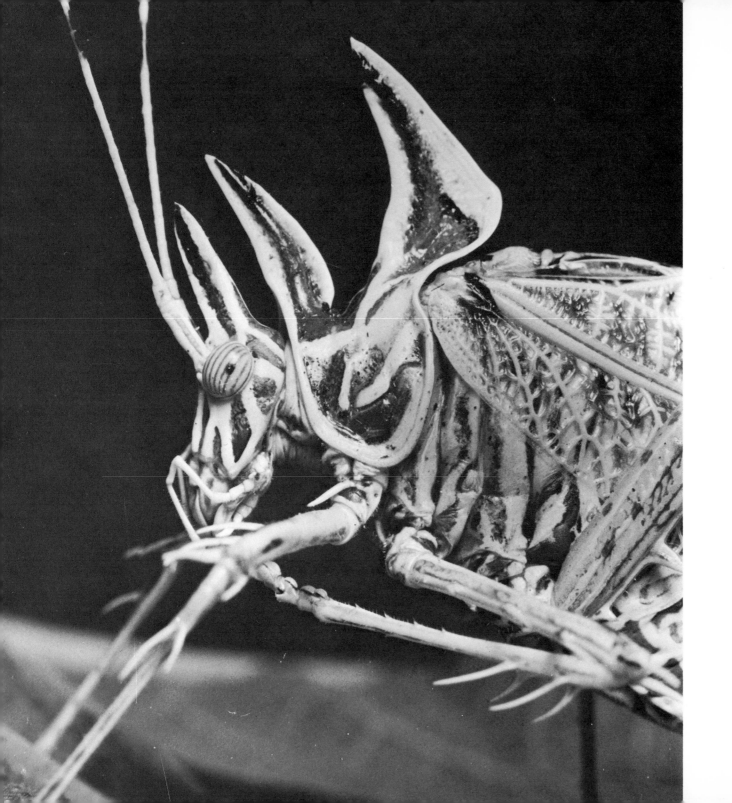

Portrait of a Peruvian Forest Katydid
Photograph, courtesy of Edward S. Ross,
Curator, California Academy of Sciences,
San Francisco, California

In that view an imaginative artist is one who creates situations of which no one else has thought before or which have never existed or never could exist. Actually the achievement of artistic imagination could be described more correctly as the finding of new form for old content, or — if the handy dichotomy of form and content is not used — as a fresh concept of an old subject.[1]

Chapter 6

A Close-up Look
at Insect and Spider Forms

The world beneath the feet of man is crowded with such an abundant population of insect species that little has been learned in proportion to the great number that exist... and here in the insect realm lies another challenge to the artist. What secrets for art can be uncovered from the tiny jungle that exists in miniature? The artist would do well to acquire a set of extra eyes to assist him in the adventure of discovering this populous kingdom of fascinating and unusual forms. Cameras and the magnifying lens are especially appropriate to discovery in this subject area.

The diversification that is characteristic of the insect societies can be idea-fuel to the artist. The unusual form, the striking in appearance, the camouflaged, the decorative — all are here for observation by those who have the patience to search for beauty in new locations. To study insects, one must be ready to establish fresh attitudes for the accept-

---

[1]Rudolf Arnheim, from *Art and Visual Perception*, Berkeley and Los Angeles: University of California Press, 1954, pages 113-14.

ance of aesthetic form. From the ordinary viewpoint, insects may appear ugly, what with their many legs, their numerous eyes perched on top and around their head, and their armor-plated or hairy bodies that emit silken threads and various assortments of poisonous and foul-smelling liquids. In such a habitat, laws do not exist as we know them. There is only one law — survival. Yet, in this strange world beautiful forms abound. The entire world of insects suggests a fresh taste of aesthetic excitement. Here are forms that defy definition. The artist in this kingdom has an opportunity to see structure and mass according to his own rules. In a sense, he must push the frontiers of his experimentation forward, as little has been done to capture this type of information on an artistic scale.

Sources for discovering the insect societies can be found in nearly every available location on the earth, both on and underneath the surface. Turn over a large stone in the garden, or inspect the bark on a tree. Look for mounds of dirt in the grass. Check underneath leaves. Look into corners. Turn over old boards. Dig a spadeful of dirt, or walk into a field with sharp eyes ready to see beyond the top grasses. Discovery of this sort can be a marvelous experience.

One characteristic of insects is that they seem almost indestructible. Many can survive sub-freezing temperatures as well as temperatures that exceed 115 degrees. For their size, they are astounding creatures, and should not be overlooked by the seeker of art. Ants, for example, possess incredible strength in comparison to their size. They are for the most part intriguing creatures if we discount their difference in appearance from the human form. Another characteristic of many insects deals with the ability to fly. Possessing wings, they are able to travel far in search of food and shelter. It is important to learn as much information as possible about specific insects, for knowledge of this type could trigger fresh interpretations with art media. Here is a world that overlaps and intertwines within our own, yet it is completely dissimilar.

Visual Symmetry in Butterflies

Butterflies and moths are extremely beautiful little creatures. From their earliest beginnings as caterpillars, they have built-in coats of attractive construction. The external covering is decoration of a gay and unusual sort with emphasis on camouflaged patterns that merge with the surrounding landscape. Many ideas for art, particularly for weaving would be possible from the study of the caterpillar and subsequent butterfly. The surface pattern from butterfly to butterfly is unique, and each is fashioned in symmetry. The symmetry extends from wing to wing on both upper and lower sections. The coloring is subtle in many respects with blues and blacks related, as well as yellows and browns, browns and greens, and numerous other variations. Nature has succeeded her highest expectations in designing the butterfly. If an artist were to utilize the entire form as subject material, he would have excellent design elements to begin with. Many specimens remind one of the glassware creations of the twentieth century designer Louis C. Tiffany. Craftsmen of this order would do well to study the forms of the butterfly for inspiration.

Insects could serve as excellent models for the development of abstract forms, or of entirely new forms. The unorthodox nature of the many forms can open up thinking in unique directions. The role insects play in arousing artistic awareness relates to the fact that they are not part of the usual world we experience. As a result, we have a fresh vision that can perceive without bias or past conditions. We can drink the full measure of our experience. Here then, is a literally untapped source of ideas for the sharp-eyed student.

Another possibility from the standpoint of the butterfly or moth is the translucent character of the wings. Light comes through the form, thus creating a pattern highly reflective and

Portrait of a Lubber Grasshopper from Southern Texas.
Photograph by Edward S. Ross, Curator, California Academy of Sciences

Slide Preparation of the Strange Larva of an Australian Lace Wing.
Protograph by Edward S. Ross from his book "Insects Close up."

Dragonfly
Ralph Talbert

Moth
Ralph Talbert

Web of Night Orb-Weaver with Morning Dew
Photograph by Edward S. Ross, Curator,
California Academy of Sciences

In the world at our feet lives
a fascinating population of
the most unusual and visually
exciting subjects. This realm
has been largely untapped by
the contemporary artist.

often iridescent. The artist might seize upon this information and explore the principles of color transparencies and translucencies with art materials that parallel nature. The newer plastics and polymer resins might offer possibilities in this direction.

The Art in Camouflage

Camouflage is another characteristic that has seldom been explored by the artist. In nature, it is of prime importance for survival. The artist could very well utilize this principle in the articulation of an art work. Let's think in terms of colors, tones, and textures that might change ever so subtly on canvas or paper, without being *immediately apparent* to the eye. Those who experiment with pigment in terms of color-optics work with such possibilities. Like the moth that blends into the tree trunk, or the caterpillar that assumes the posture and color of the stem, forms in art can also be structured on these principles. The insect in many instances has the ability to almost vanish from the scene, and unless one knows it is there, it is likely to remain invisible. Actually, many of the subtleties that can be be discovered in nature can be incorporated into the creation of art forms.

Legs, Body Parts, and Metamorphosis

Another source of idea material that can suggest new avenues in art relates to the characteristic of multiple legs. In insects, six legs are a normal occurrence. We are accustomed to thinking in terms of two legs for man and four for our domesticated and farm animals. We might consider the possibility of more than two legs for man, and so forth. Some contemporary artists have furthered new forms for the figure and broken new ground. The interpretation of the human form in abstraction is not new to artistic expression. Picasso and other cubists dis-

jointed, simplified, and redefined the figure into fascinating aesthetic relationships. It may be that a study of insect parts could serve as a basis for original interpretations of form.

What makes insects appealing from the standpoint of the artistic eye, is the great variety of differences in appearance. Some are hairy and thorny, some hard and shell-like, while others are winged and equipped with weapons that sting or bite. Others are delicate and flimsy. Another aspect worthy of consideration deals with the metamorphic cycle. We are not looking here from a biological standpoint but in terms of visual idea material. The moth, butterfly, and many other insects progress from an egg stage, through a caterpillar stage, into a pupa stage, and culminate in the adult insect. With this in mind, consider the possibility of shedding the external shell. Some suggestions that might grow from this idea could include X ray forms. That is, the simultaneous display of the inside and the outside form; an interplay of overlapping and incased subject matter.

Some other potential ideas relate to the observation of mouth parts, especially in the case of beetles. Their scissors-like jaws or mandibles may suggest possibilities with anatomical joints and levers. The nests of certain insects, such as the honey bee, the wasp, and the insect-like spiders are visually attractive as aesthetic forms. A spider's web is an exquisite creation of linear delight. When sunlight reflects on it, or when it is wet from rain, it has added qualities to study. The trails made by beetles as they carve pathways in rotted wood can be revealing as intricate doorways to design. Some specific creatures to check on in this respect include the engraver beetle, and the black carpenter ant. With their saber-pronged jaws they chisel out gigantic cavities in wood, thus causing considerable damage. The forms that are left behind however make good subject material from the sculptural point of view. Some of the newer materials

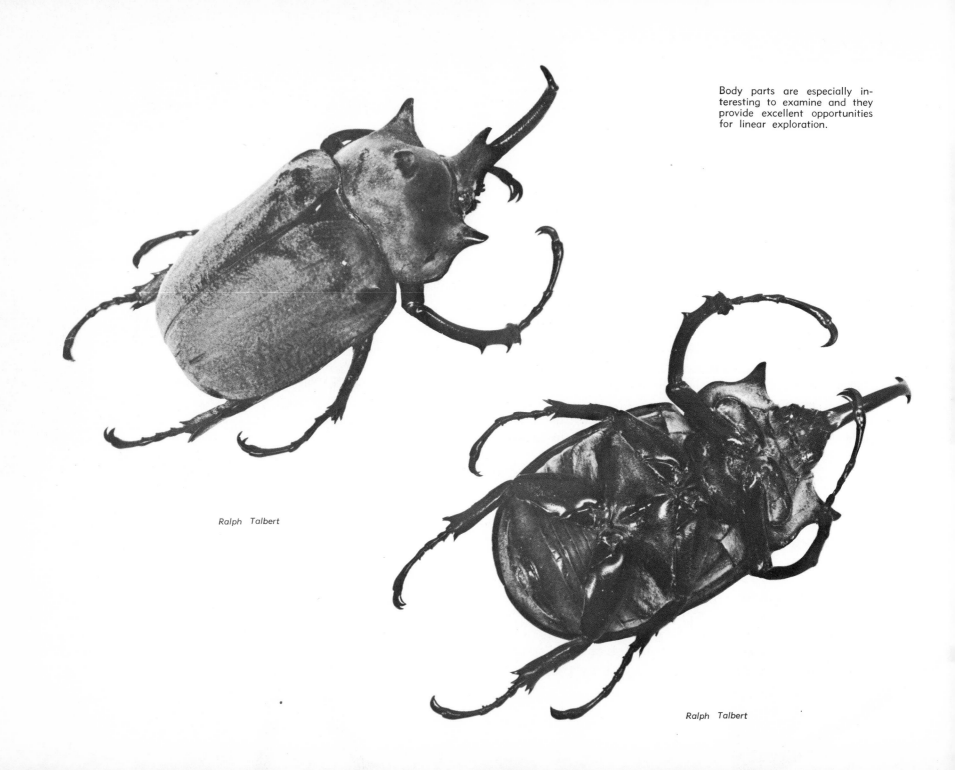

Body parts are especially interesting to examine and they provide excellent opportunities for linear exploration.

Ralph Talbert

Ralph Talbert

Tree Hopper, Amazonian Forest
Photograph by Edward S. Ross, Curator,
California Academy of Sciences

Portrait of a Californian Mantid
Photograph by Edward S. Ross, Curator,
California Academy of Sciences

Brown Lace Wing, Neutoptera
Photograph by Edward S. Ross, Curator
California Academy of Sciences

Mayfly
Photograph by Edward S. Ross, Curator
California Academy of Sciences

Milleped
Photograph by Edward S. Ross, Curator
California Academy of Sciences

When insects can be viewed at close range, a great variety of interesting detail can be explored for artistic purposes. The range of visual possibilities is almost limitless.

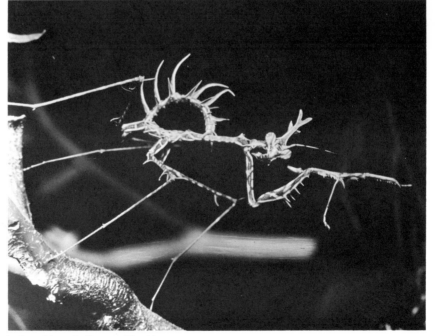

Lichen Mantid, Congo: Mt. Hoyo
Photograph by Edward S. Ross, Curator
California Academy of Sciences

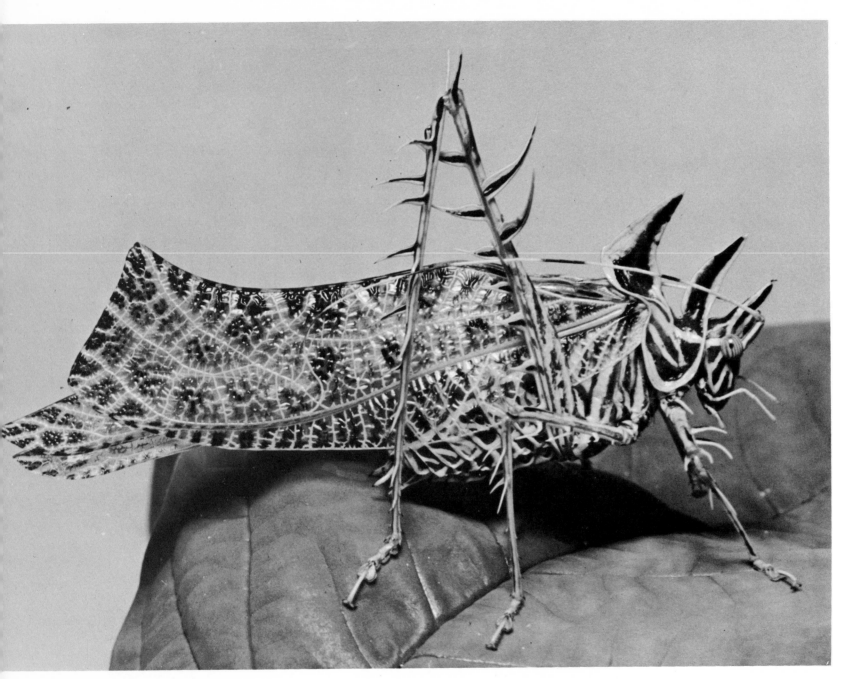

Amazonian Katydid, Markia Hystrix.
Photography by Edward S. Ross, Curator,
California Academy of Sciences

that the sculptor has been working with such as welded steel and rod, plus the acetylene torch would provide suitable media for actually creating insect forms. Metal rods are highly suggestive of insect legs and body parts, such as antennas and hairy portions.

The student of art may discover while searching for various forms in nature that a good deal of relationship exists between the subjects. For example, one might find a similar pattern in two totally different subjects. The pattern that one may discover in a leaf might also be present on the scaly back of an insect. The honeycomb made by the bee may find its partner in design in some form of marine life.

Studying insect parts close up can be a rewarding aesthetic experience. Insect eyes are more compound and much simpler than the eyes of man. In many instances, however, they can see 360 degrees. Such is the case with the robber fly. Some creatures, such as caterpillars, have very primitive eyesight and are barely able to distinguish light. Head parts on beetles are reminiscent of tanks and other defensive armor. Spiders are a merry lot when viewed under the magnifying lens. Their many sets of eyes and hairy covering make them an attractive subject for a fluid pen. It might be suggested at this point that many things in nature change their visual properties at different times of day. The subject that one sees in the morning does not appear the same in mid-afternoon or at dusk. The coloring, textural considerations and other characteristics related to the subject change with the amount of light. An artistic arrangement would have to take this into consideration.

Another aspect of the insect realm that may suggest ideas for art relates to the productivity of the species. In one nest,

Many insects display an amazingly attractive camouflage that increases their appeal from an aesthetic standpoint.

Wasp in Flight
Photograph by Edward S. Ross from his book "Insects Close up"

such as an ants' nest, or a beehive, thousands of insects live in continual close proximity to each other. They live so closely, in fact, that at times the entire conglomerate becomes a textural maze of glistening movement. Scenes of this order would be suitable for translation into art media. Tent caterpillars would offer visual possibilities, as would new-born spiders in a transparent sac.

The societies of insects are indeed fascinating realms offering much to the sensitive observer. The dragonfly is a stimulating subject, and is found in most parts of the United States. These rapid flyers can actually catch other insects while on the wing. In tropical countries, migrating army ants can strip whatever lies in their path. Survival of the fittest is a practical rule in the insect kingdom. Many an ambush waits for the unwary or unsuspecting member. All manner of traps are devised by the aggressive partners on this eternal stage. There are spider webs that are barely visible when presented against a backdrop of foliage. There are trap doors in the earth that open and close in the twinkle of an eye. Behind every blade of grass, around each pebble, fate lies in wait. From the standpoint of the hunted, there are ingenious weapons of defense. Some insects have spring mechanisms that enable them to flip over and play dead. Others squirt various liquids from their mouth to discourage the enemy. All of these factors can become source information to the artist. One must consider how he could use such data in terms of creating with art media.

Entomology journals, textbooks, and other research papers that deal with insects contain many diagrams and cross-sections that show structural parts at close range. The art student might also consider catching insects and studying them under a magnifying lens. Inventive, original configurations are possible through the study of insects as subject matter for art.

Jon Geil

For thence it is that art is born: from the lure of the elusive, the in-apprehensible, and a refusal to copy appearances; from a desire to wrest forms from the real world to which man is subject and to make them enter into a world of which he is the ruler. The artist knows that his domination is at best precarious, that its progress will be limited, yet he is conscious — passionately at first, then as the experience repeats itself, with diminishing intensity — of embarking on a vast adventure.[1]

Chapter 7

Discovery Sources from Birds and the Animal Kingdom

Birds are particularly appealing as subject material for art for they suggest a variety of directions that the artist might pursue. All birds have certain characteristics in common: They have feathers, a backbone, and only two legs. The most distinctive characteristic is feathers. These are general traits to be studied by the artist, for he must search extensively to uncover the details that explain the functional aspects of birds. Some questions to ask oneself in searching for visual information could include:

---

[1]Andre Malraux, from *The Voices of Silence,* Garden City, New York: Doubleday and Company, Inc., 1953, page 320.

Are all feathers the same size?
Are feathers soft or stiff?
Do feathers differ from bird to bird?
How does the beak attach to the head?
What is the shape of a bird's eye?
Is there an eyelid?
How does a bird turn his head?
How does he bend his neck for food?
Do all birds cling to branches?
How many claws does a bird have?
Where do the wings attach?
How does a bird fly?
Why does a bird have a tail?

These are sample questions that will aid the artistic prober in forming a basis for aesthetic ideas. If we don't learn the details of our subject, we are confined to generalities which limit idea output.

The Mechanics of Bird Flight

One amazing function of birds that has intrigued man for hundreds of years is the ability to fly. This characteristic should be observed for the ideas that may grow out of the experience. During flight, birds perform many operations aside from the basic flapping of the wings which enables them to lift into the air. Air currents are closely related to the flight patterns, and many birds, such as gulls can soar for hours on thermal currents without flapping their wings except for changes in steering or navigational functions. Other large birds of a visually attractive nature who can soar for long periods include condors, vultures, and buzzards. Some birds flap their wings more slowly than others. The larger birds have a greater span and can get the currents underneath for take-off rather easily. The hummingbird moves his wings so rapidly that the motion is barely perceptible. Most birds have a wing-flapping speed somewhere in between.

Some of the maneuvers that birds perform include soaring, hovering, diving, take-offs and landings. When birds take off from the ground they present a visually attractive example of motion. The pheasant makes a considerable amount of noise with his tremendous thrust forward. The larger birds such as cranes, herons, and flamingos actually beat their wings against the air to maintain flight. These same birds are able to use their large wingspread in the manner of a parachute during the course of landing. The air is trapped beneath their outstretched wings and acts as a braking device. Manipulation of various wing feathers controls the angle and rate of descent. There is nothing more beautiful than to see one of these large birds coming in for a landing.

There are many aspects of flight that may offer possibilities to the artist. Birds who fly in formation are one consideration. These include the migratory species who travel great distances at periodic times of the year. As a subject, such a formation could be handled within an illustrational landscape, or treated as a decorative pattern. Birds that employ diving techniques to capture their prey will be discussed shortly. There are also birds who land on water. These include ducks, geese, and other forms of waterfowl. Birds of this order have webbed feet which enable them to paddle in water and to utilize their feet as brakes when landing.

Birds of Prey

Birds of prey are well-known members of the feathered family, and include many species of flesh eaters that are found throughout most of the world. Some of the more interesting visual characteristics include the hooked bill, the strong feet that are armed with deadly talons, and the highly efficient eyes. These birds are fierce in appearance, aggressive by nature, and strike fear into the hearts of the hunted. The females are much

In studying the characteristics of birds, one must discover how the beak is attached, the surface character of the leg, the placement of the eyes, and all the parts which go to form the total experience.

Ralph Talbert

Deadly talons and hooked beaks for grabbing and tearing flesh are characteristic of birds of prey. Birds of this type make exciting subjects for exploration. They are a fearless breed who attack at will.

"Still Life" by Samuel M. Brooks
Courtesy, Crocker Art Gallery, Sacramento, California

The bird as an aesthetic form offers a wealth of intriguing material for exploration. Some artists have simplified the bird form into a subtle statement while others have considered its humorous aspects.

"Chip Off the Old Block"
by Dorothy Forbes
Courtesy, Crocker Art Gallery,
Sacramento, California

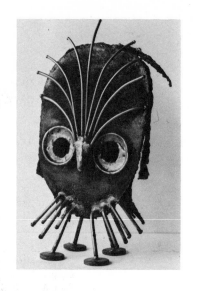

Some artists choose to interpret the same subject in many different ways. In the process, image changes with personal interpretation. Each of the owls created on this page was done by one artist, Don Herberholz of Sacramento, California.

Photographs by Barbara Herberholz

larger than the males and more aggressive. This group includes the hawks or falcons, the vultures and the various types of eagles. These birds fear nothing and will not hesitate to attack a creature many times their own size. An interesting possibility for the art student would be to experiment with a variety of media until some pleasing statements could be achieved that pertained to treatment of feathers. These birds have such fine coats and they would lend well to expressive comments with art media. Brush, ink, rice paper and materials that create a resist effect such as wax would seem suitable for this type of subject. Watercolors and melted wax work well also to achieve some striking effects. In addition to wax, other less conventional materials are also suggested, such as glues, coffee and tea grounds for coloring, and sticks in place of brushes for more unusual linear results.

Decorative Aspects and Tropical Varieties

Some birds are perfectly suited to a more decorative expression in art media. Most tropical varieties fit within this category. These birds of the jungle are usually equipped with fancy head plumes, flowing tail feathers and rich, vibrant color. They are not at all frightening or fierce in appearance in contrast to the hawks and eagles. Many birds of the tropical variety can be observed in zoological gardens and in books. One of the advantages of illustrations is that a bird can be studied at length.

The peacock could be considered as part of this particular variety, what with his extravagant tail feathers and sophisticated strut. This bird is easily accessible at most zoological locations where it can be seen happily strutting along. Another bird with an aesthetic appeal is known as the Yokohama chicken, a native of Japan. He is equipped with an enormously long tail that would be excellent subject material for a woodcut or other printing technique. Any bird forms would also be appropriate for weaving, stitchery or other craft material of this nature. Bird forms would work well in ceramic decoration. *Any* subject could be utilized with *any* medium, but some art media seem to work best with certain subjects. The artist must make his own choices in this respect.

Some highly decorated birds that are accessible in captivity include the toucon which is a native of Mexico and northern South America, and the pink cockatoo, an Australian breed of interesting variety. The parrot varieties are available in many pet shops. Many other sources for tropical birds will be discovered as one searches through books, films, pet shops, zoological gardens, and other personal contacts. Tropical birds could serve as a basis for more imaginative interpretations of bird themes. The artist might wish to exaggerate tail feathers and head dress. Unless accurate illustration is intended, a more decorative approach might be possible with this type of subject. Often, the artist can say more to express the idea of birds by interpreting in an individual style than one would find in the actual subject. In other words, the artist often starts with what he sees, and extends from that point. He *creates his interpretation* of what he sees.

Another interesting feature of birds is that they are the only creatures on the face of the earth who have feathers. For the artist they become a wonderful source of aesthetic subject material for linear or textural treatments. Feathers differ from bird to bird and there are different types of feathers on a single bird. Some birds have a complete absence of feathers on certain parts of the body while other birds are completely covered. Vultures, turkeys, and ostriches fit into the first category. Feathers serve the purpose of protecting the bird from the elements as well as becoming important navigational devices during flight. Tail feathers are usually largest and those which are located on the

Boyd Jensen

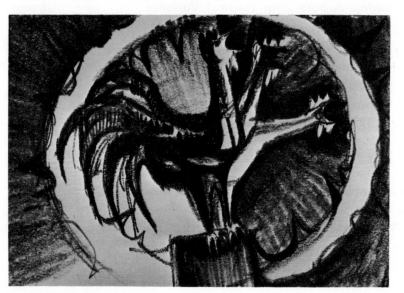

Courtesy, Crocker Art Gallery,
Sacramento, California

Boyd Jensen

breast are often tiny and soft. Coloring and decoration are present in many varieties of feathers.

Tail feathers or rectrices are usually one of the most distinguishing characteristics of birds: they appear to grow in specific shapes, including fan shape, wedge shape, lyre shape, and other pointed or rounded shapes. The lyre bird of Australia is named for his tail assemblage. Other birds possessing attractive tails include the golden pheasant, wild turkeys, peacocks, and long necked pheasants. A tail would be a beautiful subject in the hands of an artist such as Saul Steinberg who is a master with the complex linear line.

The bills of birds offer the artist a point of emphasis and should be studied carefully as aesthetic material. The bills of birds of prey are hooked and sharp in appearance. The fish-catching birds such as the pelican and kingfisher have large bills that more closely resemble a fishing-type of apparatus. As smaller birds who are not flesh eaters do not require strong bills, their bills are in proportion to their size.

The bird world is not without its humorous aspects. One delightful member who is fun to view and interesting to interpret with art media is the owl. There are the great gray owls, screech owls, short-eared owls, and many other related varieties. Owls have what is best described as a "punched-in" look; their features are bunched together on the front of the skull and project an appearance that is impish. This characteristic may relate to the fact that they perform most of their chores after dusk. Like other predatory birds who hunt living game, they possess strong legs and powerful talons. Some artists have treated the owl in great detail. Their character is so bizarre that they make good subjects in terms of sculpturing, drawing, or painting.

The question has often been raised as to the superiority of their vision. They appear to have a remarkable degree of visual acuity and can focus with amazing lucidity. It has been estimated that a bird's vision is probably ten times better than the vision of man. Birds also possess monocular vision, or a fixed eyeball that does not shift. This accounts for the staring effect, and the continual movement of the neck and head muscles in order to change the field of vision.

Wild Animals Have Visual Punch

Artistic ideas can often be suggested when one is aware enough to search for details in the subject. Only when we move beyond the generalization stage do we make more promising discoveries. In reference to wild animals, we might apply this theory to the eyes and muscles as idea sources. It might be an interesting point of departure to compare the eyes of man and of other creatures. One might wish to explore the similarities and differences between the eyes of wild animals, man, birds, insects and reptiles. In creating a composition one might draw only the eye of an animal at close range. In certain animals such as the chameleon the eyes move independently of each other so that a wide field of vision is possible. Some animals such as newts are able to see under water. Men with equipment can also see underwater. The eyes of cats and foxes have slit pupils, while lions, tigers, and other larger cats have rounded pupils. Information of this type should be "kicked around" and adapted to experimentation on canvas or in other art media.

In the realm of wild animals we can imagine many sorts of thrilling experiences. One conjures up visions of African jungles where crocodiles infest the streams and hippos linger in the mud; or we may imagine ourselves in a north woods forest where the grizzly bear is king. Lions on the prowl in search of food may invade our thoughts, while a gorilla waits on the sidelines beating his chest. When we think of wild animals we

The zoo offers an excellent opportunity to study wild animals at close range. Hundreds of studies can be made on paper during the course of a few visits.

think of something untamed, highly muscular, and extremely cunning. It is not necessary to go to the jungle in order to get information relevant to this subject. Several afternoons spent at a zoo can be rewarding for the art student. An added help would be to have a camera with a telephoto lens. Many magazines and journals on the subject provide insights that cannot be easily observed.

The muscular and body structures of various animals can also be stimulating as idea material. The anteater is a fascinating creature with a long snout, tiny eyes, and a hairy coat. The overall appearance is unusual and would adapt well to abstraction in art media. More conventional subjects such as the rabbit and squirrel have been extensively documented by the artist, and provide a subject that is friendly and light. The porcupine has an extremely hairy coat and is challenging from a textural point of view. There is some connection here with the anteater in terms of surface treatment. Monkeys are interesting animals to observe. They have hairy coats, but their features and hands are similar to those of a human. It might be rewarding to study them as aesthetic potential. Baboons are also intriguing members of the primate family. They are much more fierce in appearance. It might be an interesting conjecture to think in terms of composing a group scene that combines both monkeys, baboons, and humans. The zebra and giraffe would make excellent subject matter from a decorative point of view. Optics would also play a role with this type of subject as the artist would have to deal with tonal edges and light patterns. Many possibilities would exist here for patterns that extend from the animals to the surrounding environment. The American bison, which has now been protected on large game reserves is excellent material for the artist's brush. Here is a large sized creature with an over-sized head portion that makes a suitable subject for pleasing aesthetic forms. It has a bulky, shaggy fur

Joseph L. Horvath

"Lion" by Charles C. Nahl
Courtesy, Crocker Art Gallery, Sacramento, California

coat that might be interpreted with brush and wash, as well as pigment.

The fox, jackal, and wolf, as well as the raccoon and other members of this group could be termed beasts of prey. They have long, slender bodies and project an appearance of cunning and stealth. Their sly features would be interesting possibilities in a composition.

The Big Cats

The members of the cat family of wild beasts have both intrigued and frightened man down through history. They are beautiful creatures, muscular in appearance, and with a stance that is visually impressive. Members of this family include the lion, tiger, leopard, panther, cheetah, and the smaller related cats such as the lynx and the puma. Here are fearsome, aggressive animals that range from jungle to open plateau in Africa and Asia. These animals are good runners and excellent hunters. From a visual standpoint, they are pleasing to view. Their muscles ripple with power, and their overall appearance is one of tremendous strength. The facial features are pleasing, with large eyes, and strong contrasts. These animals are trim, and well-proportioned, thus creating an impression of speed and readiness at all times. The artist might concentrate on emphasizing the ferociousness of these cats, especially when they growl with their jaws wide open. A day spent sketching and studying at the zoo would provide much in the way of insight relating to the external characteristics of these beasts. The artist might think of the tiger or other cats in terms of various relationships. That is, the animal might be used as a symbol of aggressiveness whereby it would be compared to the force of a machine gun, an explosion, or other detonating power. If one were creating a collage, elements of this sort could be combined to establish content. The force of the cats could be played against a background of opposite expression, such as peaceful signs and symbols of society.

Domestic Animals

Another source of idea material for the art student can be found in domestic animals such as horses, dogs, cats, cows, bulls, and the like. These animals are readily available for study. The horse is a large, vertebrate creature that has a beautiful aesthetic form, is well-proportioned and muscular, and possesses a strong, modeled head. Horses are of different varieties, including the sleek racing horse, the giant plow horse, and ordinary type used for riding. A combination of first-hand experience and photographs will provide the artist with much in the way of opportunity to sketch and otherwise study horses as subject material. The artist should search for insights relating to the stance of a horse, muscle structure, facial construction, tapering of the legs, and the description of tail and mane. The horse makes a wonderful subject in terms of art expression. The forms are proportionate, shapely, and pleasing to the eye.

One never quite knows when an aesthetic spark will hit. The artist must search far and often in order to develop a backlog of data which will serve him well when the situation arises. This could be the case with cattle. Cattle are plodding and bulky in appearance and very few artists have shown an interest in documenting such beasts. Although the stripped skull, bleached white by the desert sun has often served as fine subject material, the live head as subject could also be challenging. On location study would be necessary, of course, although illustrational material could help to fill in the blanks.

Domestic cats are pleasing creatures that make fine subjects. They are small in scale, furry, soft, and available. They are also graceful, "purry," and have a soft, well formed face. They relate to the wild cats in external appearance but are much less muscular and stately. The cat has a sensitive linear form and lends well to watercolor or graphic media. Persian and Siamese cats make especially good subjects. Cats would serve well as subjects for illustrative or abstract treatments. It might be interesting to explore the ways in which the cat as subject could be varied from its original form. We might think in terms of elongation, furriness, or facial variation. The question of how to best handle the expression of *fur* is a consideration here.

Dogs have aesthetic possibilities also, and there are many varieties from which to choose. There is a good deal of range in terms of external appearance from the muscular dogs of the boxer and great Dane variety to the spaniels and other smaller breeds. Dogs such as the great Dane suggest stateliness and strength, while the poodles serve more as decorative emphasis. It would be worthwhile to discover the difference between the breeds and to learn the anatomy of each.

Examining the parts leads to a more complete understanding of the whole. It permits a concentrated focus on specific aesthetic detail that otherwise may go undetected.

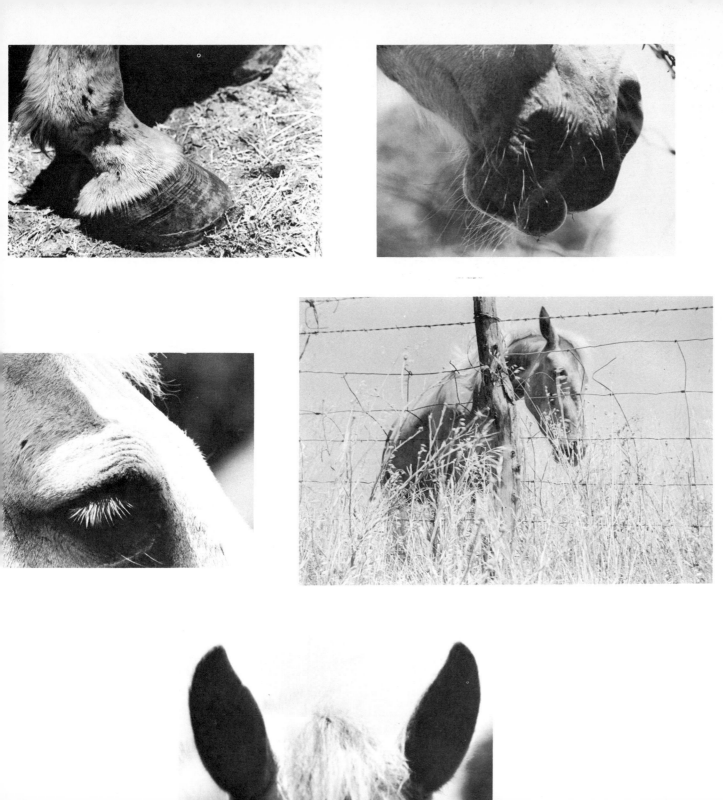
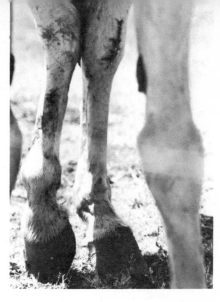

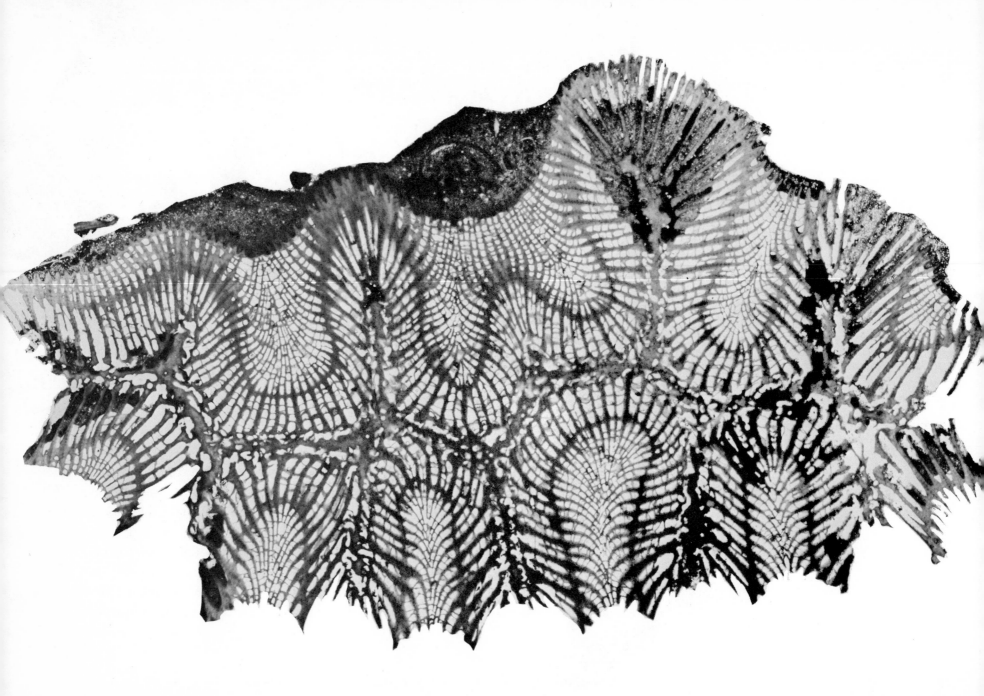

"Fossil Coral, pliocene
Courtesy, Dr. Richard S. Boardman and Frederick J. Collier,
Smithsonian Institution, Washington, D. C.

The true artist is the grindstone of the senses; he sharpens eyes, mind, and feeling; he interprets ideas and concepts through his own media. In the midst of vast social controversies he cannot escape that task. He has to take sides and proclaim his stand; indeed the artist has a formative ideological function, otherwise his work would be only an exercise of skill in composition.[1]

Chapter 8

Skeletal Frameworks as Idea Potential

The skeletal structure of vertebrate creatures provides an opportunity to study internal organization as aesthetic potential. Bone formations and skeletal joining systems can offer much in the way of artistic relationships. The shapes of bones are subtle and graceful and bones hold a particular fascination which may be attributed in part to their primary function of supporting the frame. Through observation and investigation of the skeletal structure the artist is able to relate internal format with surface articulation in order to combine the two into a cohesive relationship. Museums and college science and art departments have slides and illustrated material to provide a wide source of reference for this type of exploration.

---

[1]L. Moholy-Nagy, from *Vision in Motion*, Chicago: Paul Theobald and Company, 1947, page 29.

Fossils

The impressions that have been left in ancient rocks offer the art student solid grounds for hunting aesthetic forms. These impressions, known as fossils, range from the tiniest cellular life all the way to the larger animals such as the elephants, tigers, and the animal and plant forms that we are familiar with today. In many instances animal bones have petrified and remain as mute evidence of a world that existed millions of years ago. Other forms no longer remain but their fossilized impressions have been left in the hardened lava and organic material that has long since petrified. In coal, slate, amber, and in many other forms of ancient rock are found the traces of another age. Here we find insect evidence, leaf patterns, impressions of birds and lizards, and even evidence of mammillary creatures.

Another aspect of fossils is that a once three-dimensional form has been flattened into an impression which appears in low relief, and in many cases is merely an abstraction of its original form. We can observe the image of a form, often complete in its many details — preserved in antiquity; a rich idea source for the artist. This type of visual information would seem pertinent to anyone working in a pliable material, such as the surface of a ceramic bowl. Ceramics in particular would provide an avenue of contact for the expression of ideas derived from the study of fossils. Any type of expressive statement in linear content would suit this subject area. Art media such as brush, pen and ink, or pigment work well for sources of this kind.

In addition to finding ideas in biological and other scientific journals, first-hand discoveries can also be made and brought back for examination and eventual translation into visual media. Shale beds or locations where slate rock can be found usually offer some fossil specimens. Marine specimens impressed in rocks that have washed to shore can be found on ocean beaches.

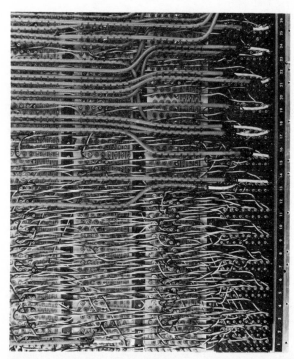

Detail of Data Processing Machine
Courtesy, International Business Machines Corporation, White Plains, New York

The visual relationships of highly dissimilar subjects indicate an internal rhythm of forms. Opposites are often brought into aesthetic harmonies through art media.

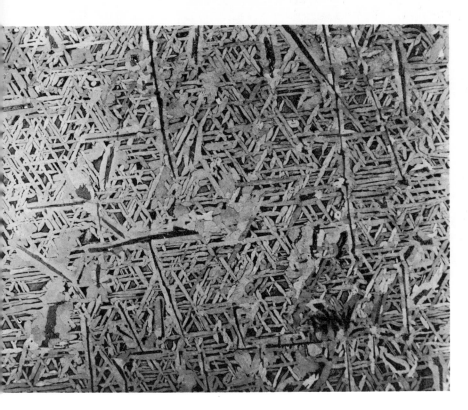

Fossil Bryozoa, Deronian Age
Courtesy, Dr. Richard S. Boardman
and Frederick J. Collier,
Smithsonian Institution, Washington, D. C.

Grant, New Mexico meteorite.
Cut Surface, Polished and Etched
Courtesy, Dr. Richard S. Boardman
and Frederick J. Collier,
Smithsonian Institution, Washington, D. C.

Radiograph of Bird of Paradise Flower
Courtesy, Eastman Kodak Company

The La Brea tar pits near Los Angeles, California, have yielded one of the largest collections of fossilized remains. Animals that roamed this country millions of years ago ventured into these pits, were caught by the tar, and sank. Their petrified bones have been extracted and are preserved in museum collections. In Arizona, the petrified forest is an example of how trees have gradually turned to stone. An interesting fact here is that all fossils were once living organisms. This fact might be worth turning around as possible idea material.

Some of the strangest creatures that man has ever observed, and then only from fossilized remains, include the family of dinosaurs. These creatures were unlike any other that we know. They are interesting from the standpoint of their size; scale alone can be impressive, although certainly not the only factor in life or art. Dinosaurs present a perfect subject for linear construction as well as an opportunity to see through the form. The reconstructed bones are valuable sources for the study of the relationship of aesthetic shapes. The view through the rib cavity of the larger dinosaurs is intriguing. Skulls of various animals have long been a subject of the art classroom.

In all forms of life, whether they be organic, vegetable or animal, we find certain relationships occurring. The skeletal structure, for example, of the vertebrate animal can be observed as an echo on a simpler scale in the leaf structure of a plant. The same similarity may be evidenced in marine forms, or in a form constructed by man. A common thread pervades all that we discover. In the most opposite of subjects, relationships occur. For the artistic person, being able to see such relationships or possibilities is an important part of developing artistic awareness. The artist must search for cues that will help him decide what is essential for his discoveries. In this sense, a sharpened focus is a necessary requisite to idea growth, for in the images that we experience lies the basis for our aesthetic expression.

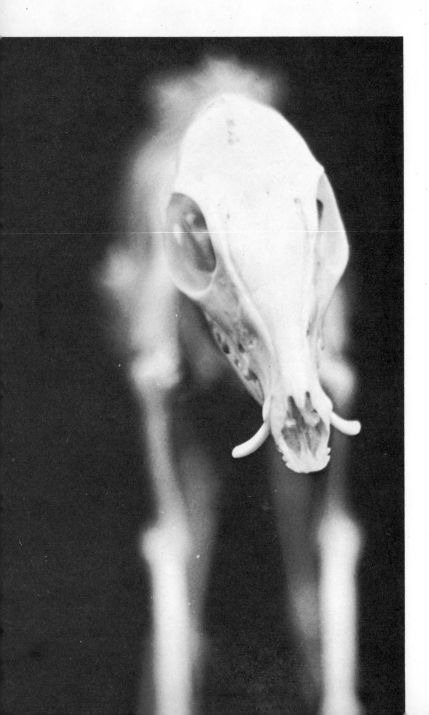

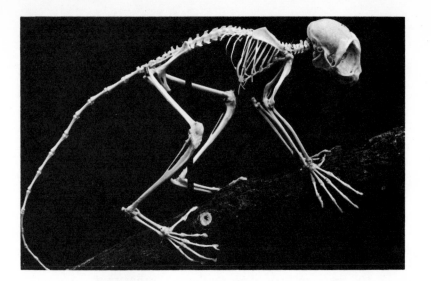

Skeletal structure can be seen as well as felt. All forms have a supporting base of one kind or another. Understanding this factor is essential to artistic creation.

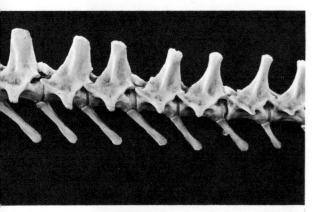

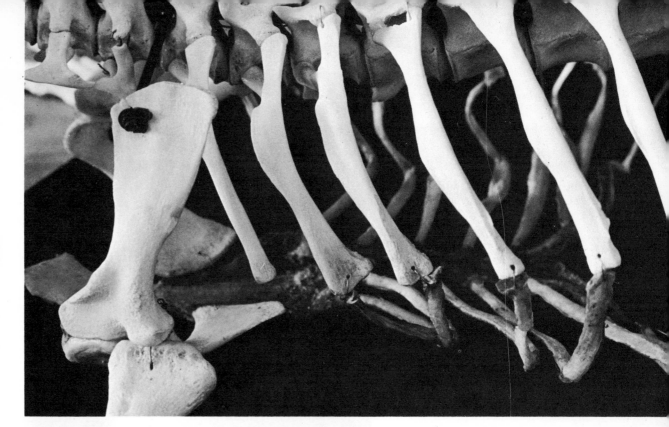

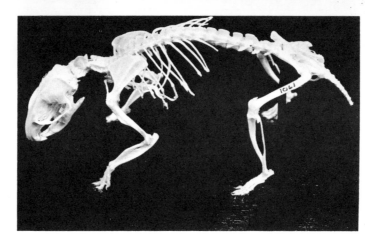

The artist then, is a sparkplug, ready to make contact with his every encounter in the visual world. Seeing something once, twice, or even half a dozen times may not be enough. Many studies and interpretations of the subject are usually required before the final statement can emerge.

Science laboratories are excellent sources for obtaining subjects. They usually have an extensive collection of various sized skeletal structures which range from birds, to bears, to man. An interesting characteristic of skeletal formations is the subtle variations that are present in bones. Some are round and have a cylindrical structure. Many bones taper gradually and have a slight twist, depending on the length of bone and its position. The bones of the rib cage, for instance, have a flattened side, and curve in a striking pattern. The skeletal structure of vertebrate creatures often reminds one of spiders, and insects that have not been reduced to the internal skeleton. Snakes have a beautiful assemblage of bones. Repetition and symmetry of design are most apparent in subjects of this nature.

In fish, the skeletal form is an exciting combination of tapering bones that set the style for the outer shell. The flatness of the bone formation of the fish has an appeal for the artist inasmuch as the bones do not curve around to meet each other. The best method of observing this characteristic is to buy a fish and cook it until the meat falls from the bones. The bones are connected to the spinal column, and will lift up in one piece if care is exercised in the removal process. In this instance, we are concerned only with the supporting structure of the fish, minus the flesh and operating features.

In searching for details within the larger form, aesthetic focus is often sharper. Many artists utilize this approach: they select choice details of the larger scene. If an artist were doing a landscape, he would choose only those portions that would fit his purpose.

As artists we should be constantly in search of visual information that will wrench the eye and stir us with possibilities that we may see in the subject. In searching for the potential that is in skeletal structures, we hope to discover ideas that will set our thinking on fire.

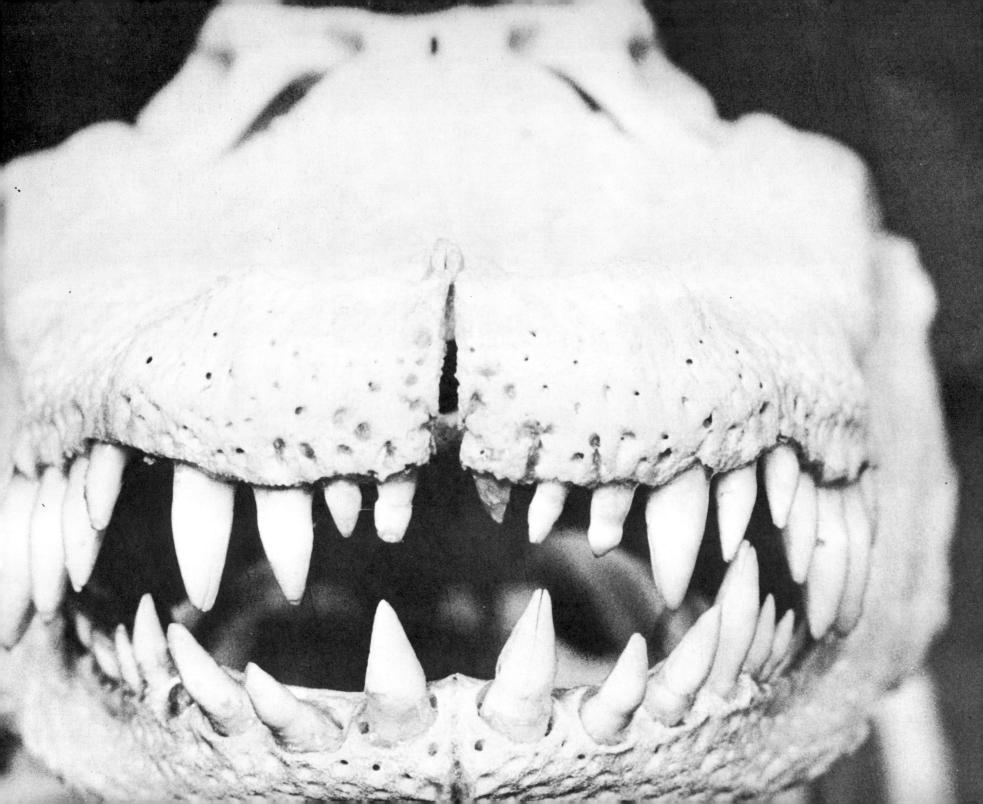

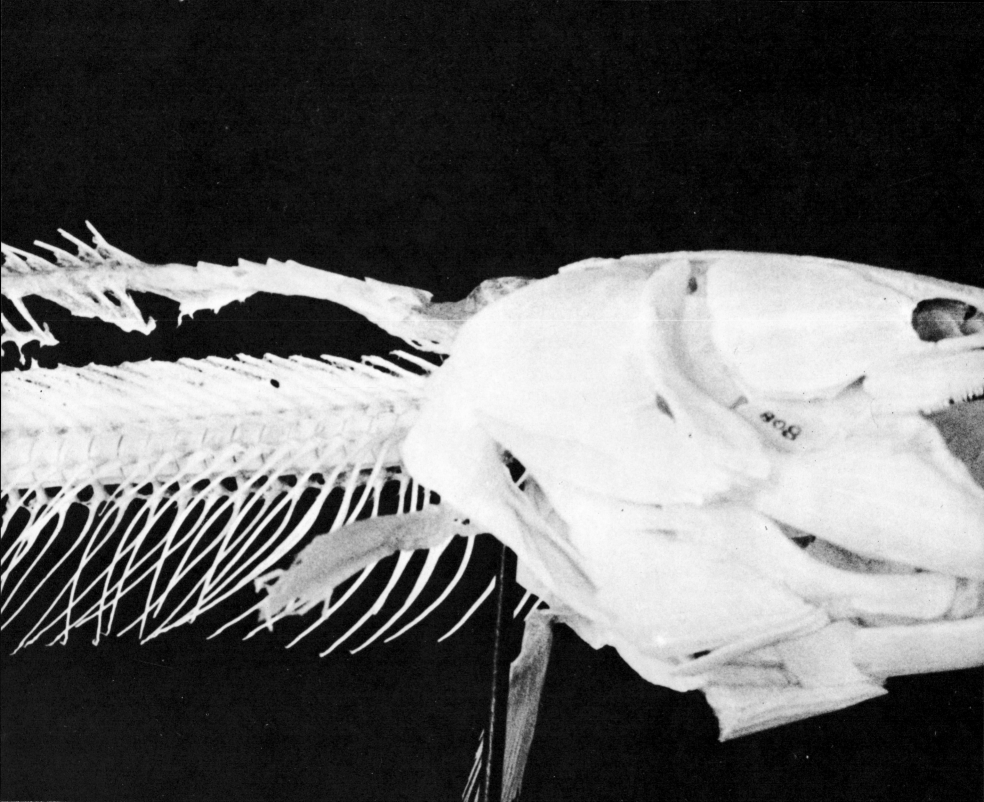

Reproducted from Moire Kit #70,719, by permission of Edmund Scientific Co., 101 E. Gloucester Pike, Barrington, New Jersey

Walnut

Boyd Jensen

Thus, during all the times of man's existence, man's imagination has been in constant alertness in the search for the secrets of all things. Constantly it has been in constant movement like the waves of the ocean with their constant birth and extinction — and constant wondering.[1]

Chapter 9

Artistic Forms from Magnification

Breath-taking worlds can unfold before the artist's observation through the use of magnification. Both the macroscopic and the microscopic universe can be infinitely enlarged for study and for the out-folding of fresh artistic vision. Under the revealing lens, daring new idea sources can be brought into focus.

There are several methods of enlarging the diminutive landscape around us. One simple means is to obtain an inexpensive magnifying glass of a type ordinarily used for reading. Objects take on a different appearance when enlarged, and details can be detected that would otherwise go unnoticed. When using a magnifying glass, one is much better equipped to detect and observe the inside of a flower, the body structure of an insect, the textural quality of a seed pod, the porousness of skin, or the external components of the human eye. Another means for examining tiny forms is through films which reveal details

---

[1]From Eliel Saarinen, *Search For Form*, New York: Reinhold Publishing Corporation, 1948, page 316.

of plant life, insect forms, and microorganisms in nature. Motion picture film allows the eye to witness astounding sequences that would be lost to normal vision: through time sequence photography, the camera can capture the complete unfolding of a flower, the mechanics of a bird in flight, or the flow of blood through an artery. Slides offer a stimulating view of cellular life. The microscope enables one to observe living cells, structural qualities of various subjects, and to discover forms that are otherwise invisible. All of these methods are usually available through high school and college libraries, science laboratories, and audio-visual departments. These aids to vision serve as another continuing reference point for enriching the imagination and opening new doors to the development of our artistic sense.

Seeing the World with Larger Eyes

From an aesthetic viewpoint there are many aspects within the macroscopic world that are available to the artist and visible to the eye. However, many forms must be searched for by giving closing attention to what is observed. We may not always know what we are after, but we can start at a specific point or "probability zone" for discovery. An area that offers new directions is that of edible items, such as potatoes, popcorn, rice, or pretzels. Each of these subjects takes on a new form when viewed from close-up. As their size is not unusual, one tends to overlook possibilities. Through the magnifying lens, however, popcorn has an appearance that is similar to pebbles on a beach; instant rice resembles tiny particles of ice or larvae; pretzels are similar to wood in appearance; the surface of raisins takes on a rugged character. Many objects have a surface that is pleasing and attractive when enlarged. Crackers have a texture that may resemble the surface on the moon. Walnuts, cereal, drinking straws — any item becomes aesthetic potential through magnification.

Slicing through different objects, such as oranges, vegetables, lemons, wood, and getting to the inside surface is another means to see the beauty of structure. Under magnification, we increase the number of aesthetic cues that are available. Any subject could serve as fuel for art: a door handle, a dresser knob, gear parts, spark plugs, typewriter keys, the weave of fabric, and the surface of anything that is growing. Our subject can be anything that we can magnify and focus on.

Artistic Vision Through the Microscope

The microscope can provide the artist with an extensive amount of information that is useful for artistic processes. Much of the preliminary ground work need not be done by the artist; there is a wealth of accessible material. Scientific journals usually abound in illustrations of microscopic forms. A description of terms will provide the idea searcher with an understanding of the tools necessary to bring the world of miniature into focus. The simplest tool for the observation of a tiny object is the magnifying glass. This is hand-held with magnification of 30 times the size of the object. This type of lens can be carried on location and provides a point of focus. A sketchbook should also be carried to note down ideas and make preliminary drawings. For stronger magnifications, the artist must go to the microscope, and to photographs. The range of most microscopes is from 1,000 to 2,000 times actual size. This is adequate for most discovery sources. The more recent electron microscope provides for magnification that can reach over one million times normal scale. This means that forms never before dreamed of by the scientist or artist can come into view. Forms photographed at this extreme range are available in the scientific journals, and also in slide form where they can be projected on a screen and studied at length. Many sources for art ideas can be obtained by going through back issues of science journals and examining the photographs in terms of design properties and other aesthetic considerations.

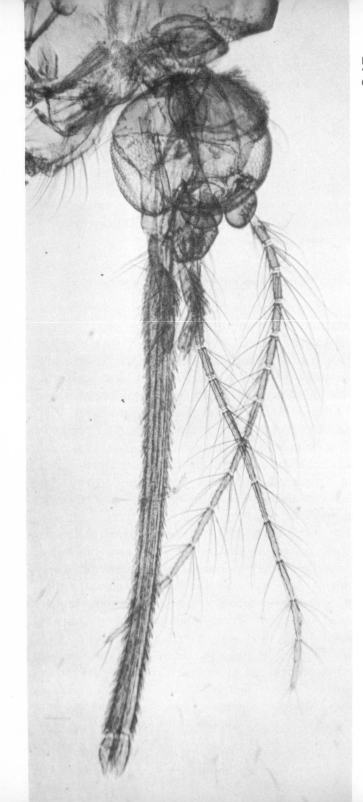

Photomicrograph: Growth of Secondary Eye of a Bathylychnops Exilis; a "Four-eyed Fish"
Courtesy, Dr. Ole Munk

When we are able to enlarge our world through technical aids, the range of aesthetic possibilities is multiplied for an entirely new way of seeing is available.

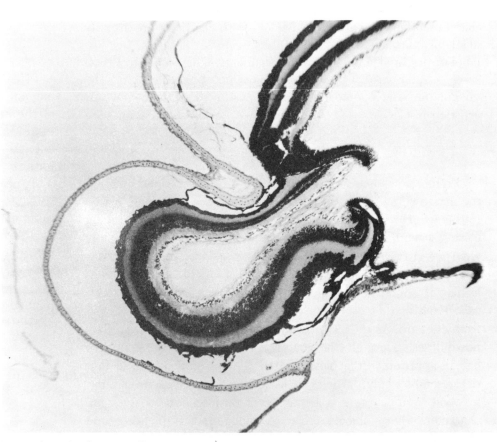

Photomicrograph of a mosquito
Courtesy, Eastman Kodak Company

Cereal

Instant Rice

Unpopped popcorn

Photographs by Boyd Jensen

Pine cone

Raisins

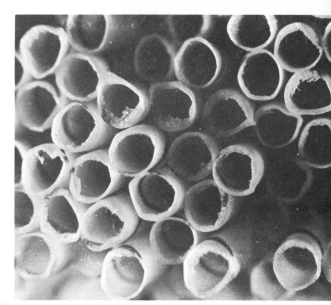

Drinking Straws

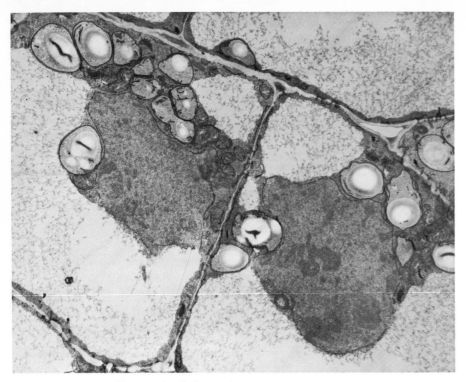

Electron Microscope Photograph of Cotton Integument
Photograph, courtesy of Lee Kavaljian

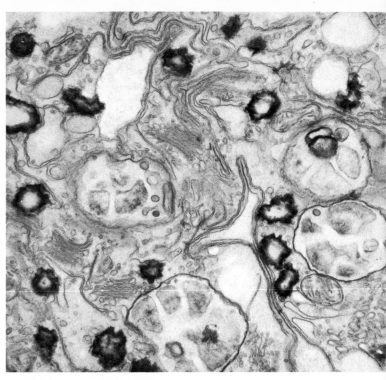

Electron Microscope Photograph of Pollen Tube
Photograph, courtesy of Lee Kavaljian

Photomicrograph of Cross-Section of
Inner Bark of Grand or White Fir
Photograph, Courtesy of U. S. Forest Service,
Forest Products Laboratory,
Madison, Wisconsin

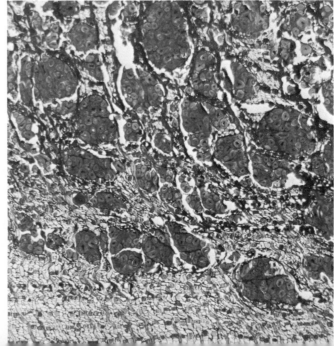

An Inside View of Cellular Life

Rock formations and rock components are highly fascinating when viewed under magnification. Some rocks indicate extensive evidence of marine life and other organisms of a past age, i.e., marine limestone. Other rocks are crystalline, and one can see the wonderful effect of transparency, translucency, and reflections that are similar to those found in ice formations or other frozen substances. Microphotographs of various substances offer the artist new insights into design sources and aesthetic structures.

Algae, which are found in water, contain many attractive forms and structures. The varieties are almost infinite and a person who is searching for beautiful symmetry will find much to his liking in this microscopic wonderland. Marine diatoms are a particularly attractive group of algae because of the numerous types and patterns.

Seed plants under the microscope offer some sophisticated visual information which the art student can utilize as idea material. Cross sections of twigs and other plant growth are visually powerful. Cellular composition of plant material is often mosaic in character and highly decorative in surface articulation. Microscopic material of this order has a splendid surface texture that can be photographed and recorded for future use.

Viewing bodies of insects under magnification can be a stimulating experience. Unique and little seen forms can be revealed. Head parts, such as eyes and mouth would seem especially appropriate for investigation. Some insects that would offer exciting possibilities for visual expression include grasshoppers, beetles, and bees.

Transparencies of Visual Form

Through magnification and the marvel of the electron microscope, inside and outside structure can be revealed for examination by the artist. An opaque substance, such as a tree trunk, or a nautilus shell can be exposed to our examination and the inner structure can be viewed in detail. Transparency, through the techniques of radiography, can reveal human form such as muscular structure, tissues, and bones within the same visual sequence. The entire structure of an organism can be exposed for visual experimentation. Shells, trees, leaves, and animal forms — both the inside and the outside — can be viewed simultaneously. Through such techniques as radiography and the electron microscope our horizons for art have grown wider and deeper, and we are encouraged to build new images from these foundations.

Cameras are Aesthetic Storage Chambers

Both motion picture cameras and still cameras are significant aids to the development of artistic awareness. They assist the artist in capturing information of a vast range and nature. Motion that can not be witnessed with the human eye can be recorded easily with the camera. The artist can gather art idea sources even though the information will not be utilized for some time: through film, the artist has his personal storage vault which he can draw from whenever he is ready. Information can be recorded dealing with birds in flight, the complete cycle of a flower, animals running at high speed, motion in the dark, and any high speed action such as the path of a bullet or the pattern of a drop of water. Much information that occurs within our visual frame of reference cannot be studied because of the rapid motion involved. The camera is able to stop any action at any point, so that patterns and visual cues become available for observation and study.

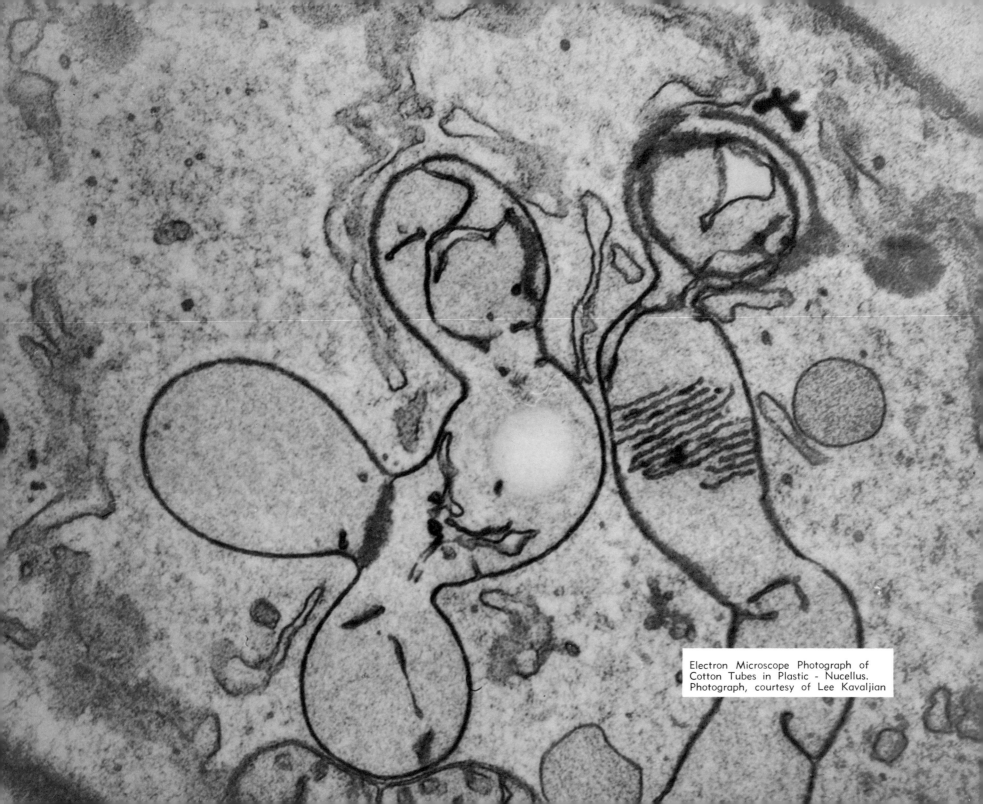

Electron Microscope Photograph of
Cotton Tubes in Plastic - Nucellus.
Photograph, courtesy of Lee Kavaljian

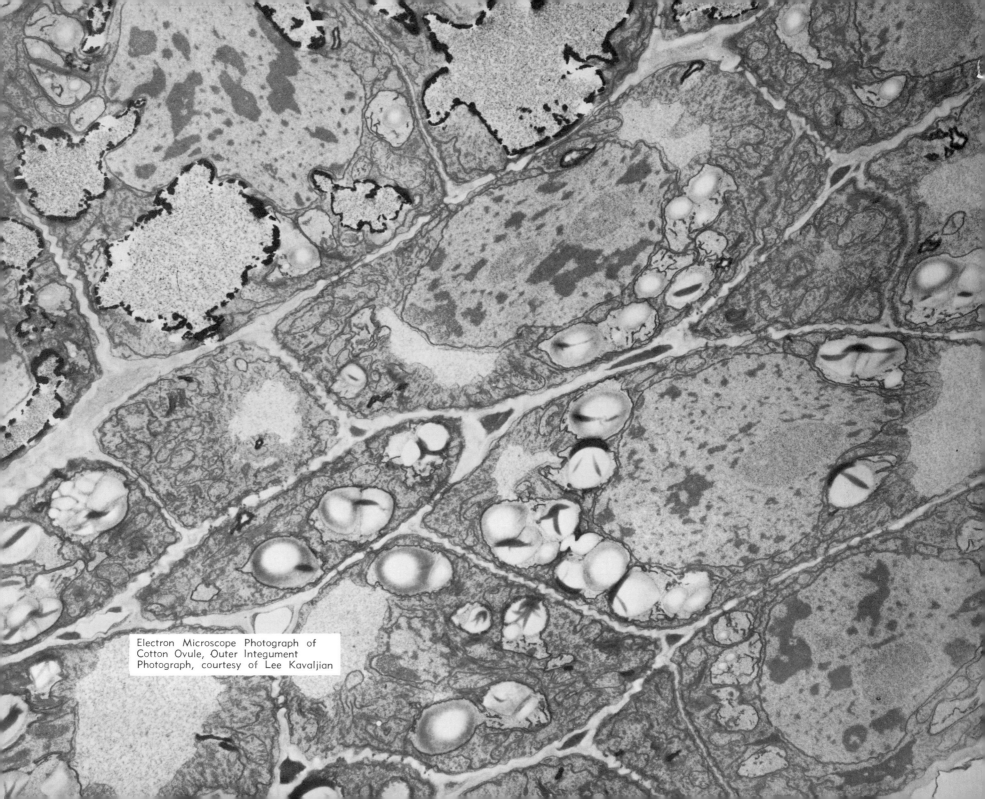

Electron Microscope Photograph of
Cotton Ovule, Outer Integument
Photograph, courtesy of Lee Kavaljian

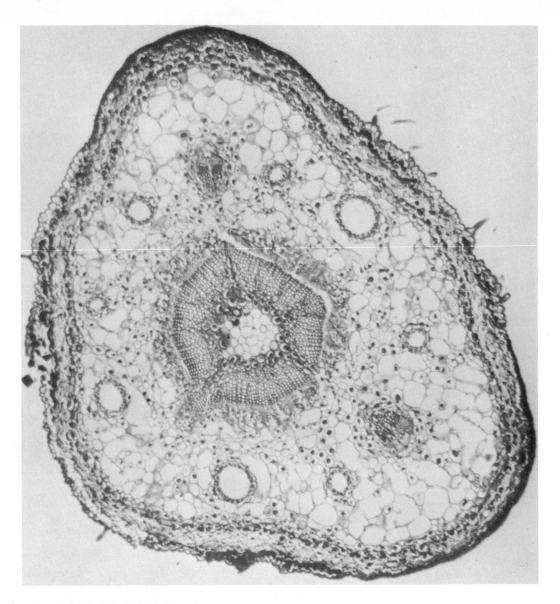

Photomicrograph of Radial Section of
Inner Bark of California Torreya or California Nutmeg.
Courtesy, U. S. Forest Service,
Forest Products Laboratory, Madison, Wisconsin

The camera enables the artist to go back over the subject many times in the privacy of his studio or work area and select those parts that have meaning for the specific intent. It also permits the artist to gather much more information than he could by sketching on the spot. Of course he should continue to sketch and to take photographs and use both for further study.

Photomicrograph of Transverse Section of
Red Oak Showing Three Growth Rings.
Courtesy, U. S. Forest Service,
Forest Products Laboratory, Madison, Wisconsin

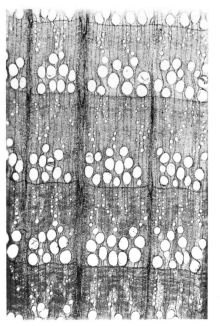

Photomicrograph of Cross-Section of Young Branch of Douglas Fir.
Courtesy, U. S. Forest Service, Forest Products Laboratory, Madison, Wisconsin

When one can extend his vision his awareness for life and art is greatly increased.

Nature is the formless source of all forms, and yet it remains unaffected by its forms.
Thus it appears to us as if mysterious.
No matter how closely we scrutinize its coming toward us, we cannot discover a beginning.
No matter how long we pursue it, we never find its end.[1]

Iph Talbert

Chapter 10

Triggering Art Ideas
by Observing Sky and Land Forms

The landscape has been an artistic paradise since the dawn of painting; every conceivable challenge that exists in a subject is present. The land, sky, and the water offer so varied a selection for the creative eye that this type of subject shall always remain as a significant source of aesthetic expression. There is nothing quite like sweeping one's gaze over a vast panorama of land. Sometimes it is fruitful to sit with no particular aim in mind, and scan the terrain. Sitting on a rise can provide one with a view of the land below. The patterns caused by the farmer's plow and the crops create an intriguing rectangular arrangement, with curving streams and tree foliage breaking into the pattern. The artist, be he painter, sculptor, or craftsman sees in the landscape what he has learned to see. Here is a statement by the French painter, Corot:

---

[1]*Tao Teh King,* by Lao Tzu. Interpreted as *Nature and Intelligence* by Archie J. Bahm, Frederick Ungar Publishing Co., New York, 1963, XIV, page 21.

The nocturnal vapours are still creeping in silvery flakes over the frozen green of the grass. Ah! A first ray of sunshine. The tiny flowers seem to wake up happily. Each has its tremulous dewdrops. The leaves shiver with cold in the morning breeze. Invisible birds are singing beneath the leaves. It seems as though the flowers were saying their prayers. Little butterfly winged cupids frolic over the meadow, making the tall grass ripple. One sees nothing. Everything is there. The whole landscape lies behind the transparent gauze of the fog that now rises, drawn upwards by the sun, and as it rises, reveals the silver spangled river, the fields, the trees, the cottages, the further scene.[2]

Observing the Terrain with Sharp Eyes

Land patterns and various visual relationships emerge when one is able to view the land from several vantage points. Oftentimes, the slope that one is standing on can be used for the foreground in the actual composition. Another interesting possibility for discovering land forms is to lower oneself to near ground level or to view land from below while looking upward. This places the horizon well above eye level and provides a more unusual relationship. Looking up or down a slope can offer many possibilities for artistic arrangements. When we view the land from above, we can pick out the field patterns, the pathways of creeks, and existing landmarks. Here we have a wonderful collage; a piecing together of shapes that are both rectangular and square, and are bisected by levies and other natural and artificial interruptions which cut a swath through the land. In many parts of the country, we have a range of vision that extends far into the distance. A related factor in discovering land patterns has to do with close-up observations of the grasses and grains that cover the land. These can be treated in terms of textural surfaces or linear movements that lead the viewer in and through artistic space.

Sky and Clouds

The eye might begin an aesthetic search with soft billowy clouds which move silently across the sky in thunder-like crescendos. These nebulous forms offer many possibilities for imaginative configurations. Some clouds are massive in appearance while others are thin and streaked. Some are dark and others are marshmallow white. Thunderclouds and storm clouds are especially appealing. An appropriate time to draw or paint the sky is when the large clouds are massing for a coming storm. The imagination needs little stretching at such a time. Sometimes the darkness of the sky can provide a contrast with the lime green or gold of the fields below. Geographical location may have some bearing on the appearance of the sky. In some sections of the country the sun is especially strong and shines brilliantly all summer. In other sections of the country, clouds hold the upper hand.

Most of us have seen a brilliant blue sky without a cloud in sight. The time of day plays a considerable role in the ever-changing atmosphere of sky. A haze of dust or smog in the air will greatly affect our impression. Interpreting the sky need not be done in terms of what is actually there: the sky may be interpreted in an individual manner. There is little need, if we consider the imaginative viewpoint, to paint the sky a pastel baby blue. Sky can be of any color, depending on the mood the artist wishes to reflect. Just as we associate gray skies with rainy days, we can associate exciting events with warm skies. In treating a sky with pigment, one artist might handle the sky with a soft, flat stroking of the brush so that one smooth tone emerges. Another artist may interpret the same sky with whip like slashes and huge globules of pigment thrust on the canvas to create a feeling of action. Clouds can be a valuable cue for the artist and provide him with the means to articulate the vast plane of the sky into a meaningful form. Clouds can

---

[2]Friedenthal, Richard, *Letters of the Great Artists*, New York: Random House, Inc., 1964.

The seeker for beauty must search both the distant landscape as well as the immediate terrain; the winter sky as well as the summer haze.

Ralph Talbert

Ralph Talbert

Nick DeLucia

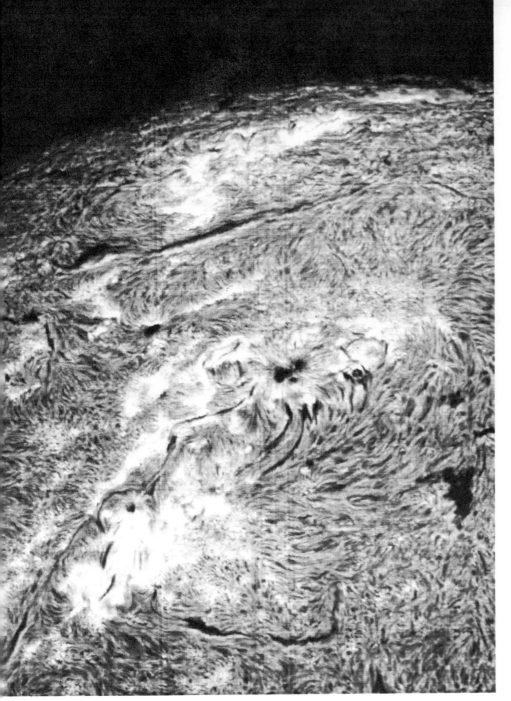

Spectroheliogram in Red Light
Courtesy, Mount Wilson and Palomar Observatories

"Bay at Sunrise" by Dong Kingman
Courtesy, Crocker Art Gallery, Sacramento, California

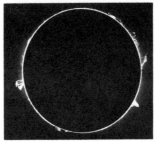

Whole Edge of Sun
Courtesy, Mount Wilson
and Palomar Observatories.

Scientific journals of various types can be a valuable source for compositional possibilities. Astronomical laboratories have excellent collections of visual masterpieces appropriate for aesthetic considerations.

"Folsom Lake, California" by Earl Linderman

be handled as soft curvilinear forms, or they can be wispy, airy and filled with transparency. They can be high flying streaks of white on a blue field, or they can be a dark, ominous low hanging blanket of gray cover. Clouds might be in the form of fog with the appearance of a blanket of white rolling in to cover the landscape. Fog clouds are mysterious and exciting.

Atmospheric Fog and Mist

When the fog moves in over the landscape it drops a silver curtain and makes bright things dark and mysterious. Much of what is partially hidden by the fog and mist becomes potential for the artist's imagination; the sharp edges become blurred, and the square corners have a fuzzy edge. In an extremely heavy fog, everyday forms take on new magic; an expectancy; a feeling of suspense. Some artists have interpreted fog in a nostalgic manner. The American romantics, George Inness and Albert P. Ryder, were fond of creating atmospheric effects viewed at night or in the mist. Some subjects such as boats, harbors, bridges, and lights of the city seem well suited to misty, atmospheric landscapes.

Observing Bright Sunlight and Shadows

In bright sunlight, one experiences the sensation of warmth and growth. Bright sunlight may occur at various times of day and under varying temperatures. The subject may include glare where extreme light combines with shadows on white fields of snow. Sunlight in summer mingled with blue skies and green fields creates a different impression than sunlight in winter, and one must interpret accordingly. Sunlight may reflect intense heat and suggest a desert atmosphere or a dusty town in summer.

When one considers the sun, one must also examine shadows caused by the position and surface of objects in the path of the light rays. Shadows could be an intriguing direction for artistic exploration; noon-time shadows that are short because the sun is almost overhead, shadows in late afternoon that creep swiftly across entire fields and follow the contours of the hills. The paintings of Edward Hopper are masterful examples of the effective use of sunlight and shadows. Sunlight can create unusual patterns, as when it strikes a lattice-work fence or an iron gate. Extreme distortion occurs under conditions of artificial light, especially in a nighttime setting. In this type of environment there is little visual depth. We can view the subject that exists within the perimeter of the light source, but must relinquish the depth of field that would be possible under daylight conditions. It might be a profitable experience to view the same subject in the morning, in the afternoon, in the early evening, and at dark. The source of light and shadow could be compared and variations in the subject could suggest artistic possibilities.

Searching for the Details in the Landscape

Abstract qualities in terms of linear patterns are evident in fields of swaying wheat and grains. Grasses combine with the brilliant colors of the terrain — lime greens, olives, ochres and yellows to create magnificent possibilities for the artist. One can observe the sky and witness an unbroken flow of blue or gray; or observe a field of golden wheat as far as the eye can see; or corn stalks which extend for miles. In nature, there exist unbroken patches of color in both low and high intensity. Often, the color tone will change as we view the subject so that we must continually be alert to such changes for idea potential. Dikes, levies, stone walls, water towers, and other structures provide accents to the composition. In viewing the countryside

"Yosemite" by Thomas Hill
Courtesy, Crocker Art Gallery, Sacramento, California

The subject remains constant in nature even though change occurs at all times. Interpretation is always an individual thing. Each person will see from his vantage point and express accordingly in his art medium.

"Landscape" by Roland Petersen
Courtesy, Crocker Art Gallery, Sacramento, California

Photographs by Ralph Talbert

The face of the landscape changes ever so subtly and the artist must be aware of its moods— ready to capture scenes and moods that exist only for that period of time.

"Beal's Point, California" by Marlene Linderman
Courtesy of the artist

At dusk, or at sunrise, the terrain has an atmosphere that invites observation. The light is softer and the edges of objects become blurred and softened.

Shadows creep across forms in a silent pattern that makes the subject more stimulating. Often, the forms are exaggerated and seemingly new forms create images of visual intensity.

from the air, one experiences an entirely different situation. Here, the fields and land patterns appear to fit more like a picture puzzle. We don't have the feeling of visual depth that we experience when viewing the subject from a slope where the angle is slight. From the air we have a somewhat flattened impression of trees, barns, and roadways. Textural considerations become more significant as well as spatial relationships.

Other viewpoints include looking through grasses at close range and viewing the distant scene, and looking down mountainous country and studying rivers which cut through at the base of a valley. One works with the landscape that is available. The artist learns to find his challenges in terms of the subject at hand. A sensitive eye and an imaginative mind can turn any subject into a wealth of aesthetic material. Successful art pieces do not lie in the choice of subject, but in the expression and skill of the artist.

A close-up view of a subject might be interesting. A rock, tree trunk, patch of earth — any part of the scene could serve. There is so much to grasp and utilize in this vast world of ours. It is a big land and it beckons to the artist. Painting the landscape is quite a different experience from creating non-objective forms, or working with the figure. Each artist sees in an individual manner. The landscape is an aesthetic hunting ground that abounds with visual game of every description and variety.

Composite photograph showing moon at last quarter.
Courtesy, Mount Wilson and Palomar Observatories.

Eel larva of an unknown species captured off the Oregon coast
Courtesy, Dr. James Pearcey, Oregon State University

Form arises in many ways. Form in nature emerges from the impact of order upon order, of element upon element, as of the forms of lightning or of ocean waves. Or form may emerge from the impact of elements upon materials, as of wind-carved rocks, and dunes. Form in living things too is the impinging of order upon order — the slow evolving of shapes according to function, and drift, and need.[1]

Chapter 11

Exciting Forms
Within Waters and Seas

The Sounds of the Oceans

The large body of water known as the ocean is more than nature's mighty bathtub. To the searching eye, it is a gigantic form that is constantly in motion. Its sounds roll on and on. On a trip to the beach one can observe the breakers, the swells, and the rolling of the surf as it moves rhythmically across the field of our vision. The beauty that is known as ocean must be observed in detail, for first glances serve only to whet the appetite for more.

When one stands on the beach and observes the surf rolling in, special attention should be paid to the constant but variable pattern created by the water as it moves up the beach. Changing one's position alters the level of viewing and reshuffles the seascape into a new relationship for further appraisal. The ocean has a translucent character about it when the waves climb, and just before breaking, the light from behind passes through;

---

[1]Ben Shahn, from *The Shape of Content*, Cambridge, Massachusetts: Harvard University Press, 1957, page 68.

we know that water is transparent, but only when sufficient light is thrown upon its surface.

The sound of the ocean as it opens and closes its mighty jaws can be a stimulating thing. *Much of discovery is not by visual means alone.* The more complete feeling or knowledge of a form is richer when all of the senses play a part in the experience. The artist is better equipped to paint the ocean if he has heard its roar, tasted it and felt its chill.

Invertebrate Creatures

The forms from the waters of the world offer a wealth of visual material to stimulate artistic thinking. The invertebrates, or those animals who have no spine, include coral, sponges, jellyfish, shells, mollusks, and sea anemones. Many other forms live within the depths: there are shapes and forms that have never been touched by an artist. In many parts of the deep there is eternal darkness. A characteristic of the invertebrates is their relationship to the environment in which they live. Many of them have tentacles or openings that permit water to flow through and around them in a type of breathing sequence. Many of these creatures have thin, transparent membranes as external covering. The jellyfish, of which there are several varieties, is an excellent example. The Portuguese man-of-war has long trailing tentacles which can sting and paralyze its victims. It is exquisite in form, however, and would make solid subject matter for the artist.

Sponges are interesting because of their external form that is riddled with openings which allow the water to move in and through. Many are reminiscent of bushes or small trees, and others are suggestive of expanding creatures that crawl slowly over the surface of things. Sea anemones are especially attrac-

Ralph Talbert

tive forms of sea life. In effect, they are tiny animals that resemble flowers, yet contain stinging cells that can paralyze other creatures. Coral is another form that can be explored through photographs and actual examination. It has a skeletal type of structure that spreads in many directions and takes many forms. Mollusks, or shells, have always been appealing to the aesthetic explorer in terms of design properties and visual symmetry. The simplicity of the shell form would lend well to compositional arrangements. Starfish have interesting possibilities for the interpretation of aesthetic form. Many of these shell type of creatures can be combined into compositional relationships. The sea horse is interesting because of the positioning of the head and neck in relation to the body. It is one of the few fish forms that has its head at an angle to the rest of the body. While many of these forms of invertebrates can be discovered at the beach, other likely sources for exploration include aquariums, and illustrative material. Fish in pet shops, films, slides, and biological specimens offer other sources.

The Visual Dynamics of Fish Varieties

In searching for aesthetic cues within the waters of the world, the most likely forms to consider are the many different varieties of fish. Each style or body type offers to the artist a special form of visual treat. Fish possess a remarkable diversity of exterior forms in terms of shape, surface pattern, and color tone. Some fish are extremely long and narrow while others appear short and pudgy. Some are transparent, while others dazzle us with their brilliance. Some types, such as the barracuda and pike, are ferocious in appearance. Others, such as lion fish, puffer fish, and balloon fish, have a somewhat humorous aspect. In addition to fins, some fish possess burrs, spines, spikes, and swords as part of their surface covering. Most of these varieties can be observed in the aquariums of our

Radiograph of Nautilus Shell
Courtesy, Eastman Kodak Company

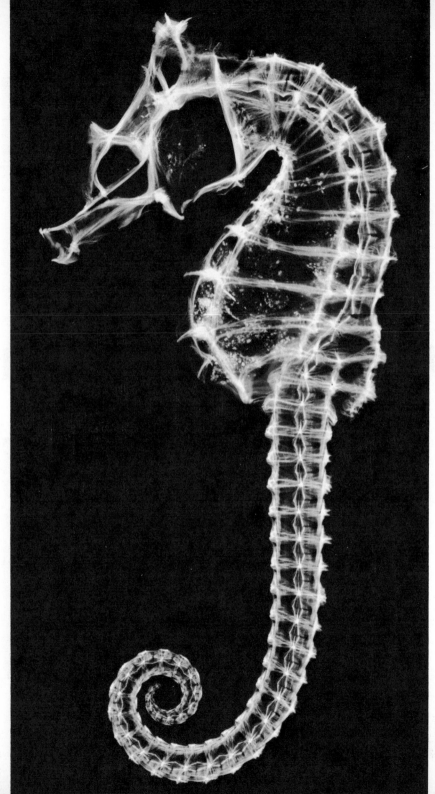

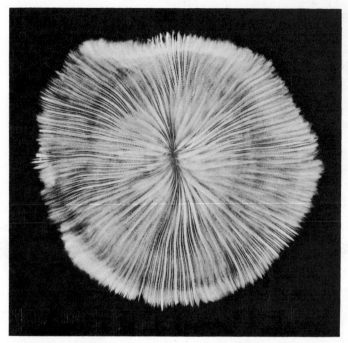

Radiograph of Shell
Courtesy, Eastman Kodak Company

Symmetry and subtlety of form are distinguishing characteristics of the invertebrate creatures of the sea. They offer graceful images that are highly stimulating. Variety is endless in the many types and species that exist in marine and fresh water bodies.

Radiograph of Sea Horse
Courtesy, Eastman Kodak Company

Ralph Talbert

Radiograph of Spindle Shell
Courtesy, Eastman Kodak Company

Radiograph of Starfish
Courtesy, Eastman Kodak Company

Today science enables us to see what was hidden from our observation in the past. Through the magic of the camera and the X ray, worlds of aesthetic adventure are opened for the artistic eye.

larger cities. Many types of fish have a glassy, jewel-like sheen that is visually attractive. Surface decoration on many varieties is varied and highly decorative. There are many bizarre designs and designers and craftsmen have long utilized such forms as subject material for weaving, jewelry, and fabric creations. Of course, the forms need not be imitated directly. Rather, they should serve as the basis for interpretation in an individual manner — abstractly or expressionistically as the artist sees fit.

The individual parts or details of fish might suggest possibilities for art. Scales, for example, make a pleasing repeat pattern and would adapt well to textural considerations in an art form. The eyes and mouth parts might be worthy of consideration. Teeth in particular are fascinating when one examines them at close range. The idea of fish traveling in schools or clusters could trigger some thinking along aesthetic channels. The tremendous mobility of fish might be an idea worth pursuing. Some types that are visually interesting to observe include the Siamese fighting fish, turkey fish, striped sturgeon, and the various kinds of trigger fish.

Amphibians and Alligators

Other interesting creatures to study for aesthetic potential are the salamanders, frogs, snakes, alligators, and others of this classification. Both the amphibians and the reptiles have an unusual visual appearance. They are fascinating, however, and offer much in the way of stimulating idea material. Reptiles in particular have a rough hide that is covered with ossified scales and a textural surface that would be artistically valuable. The entire shape of the alligator, including its irregular head and clawed toes, is appealing.

Frogs also have an attractive external shape that is well suited to aesthetic expression. Oriental artists have long utilized such subject matter. Lizards can offer much in the way of textural possibilities for their hide is tough and wrinkled. Students of drawing could have a field day with this type of subject. Illustrations of such creatures would enable the artist to focus closely on these strange beasts. Many of the creatures named herein including the alligator, lizard, and toad remind one of the age of dinosaurs. They are vestiges of forms of life that roamed the continents long before the birth of man.

Snakes offer potential as textural material and their heads are especially interesting. Many of these reptiles are frightening in appearance because of their piercing eyes and deadly jaws that can swallow objects whole. Snakes range in size from less than a foot to the larger ones such as the anaconda which reaches lengths of 30 feet or more. Many snakes as well as other reptiles and amphibians have a built-in camouflage network that helps them to blend in with their surroundings. Many snakes also have a decorative surface pattern that might offer possibilities. The diet of snakes is somewhat intriguing, and may suggest ideas for exploration. It consists of everything from man down to the smaller creatures. There reportedly are cases on record where African rock pythons have eaten humans. It might be interesting to combine a snake, alligator, and lizard into one compositional relationship. The artist has opportunities galore to draw subject material that is strange and mysterious in this bizarre realm of amphibians and reptiles. Consider the possibility of painting at close range an entire series using lizards, snakes, and alligators; perhaps only head sections enlarged to fit a six foot canvas — one head to each canvas!

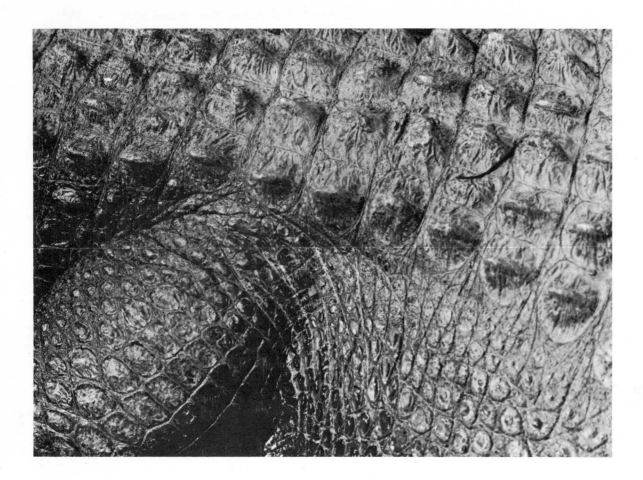

The surface quality of any subject can be an intriguing challenge to the observant person. Some surfaces are scaly and rough while others have the polished slickness of chrome steel.

Sunken Treasures as Visual Material

Other subjects that relate to oceans are the treasures and material goods of man that have been buried by plunder, war, and the elements. Spanish galleons, English frigates, and Dutch vessels — some of which never completed their maiden journey lie buried at the bottom of the ocean. Some were sunk by shore guns, some by pirate raiders; others were crushed against reefs in storms. Today they rest in their graves, encrusted with seaweed, corrosion, and the residue of time. Yet, they are still there; the masts, the anchors, cannons, chains, ripped and torn metal, treasure chests. Many stories revolve around this type of subject — lost divers, giant squid lurking in dark holds, pieces of eight scattered in the mud of the ocean bottom, and killer sharks waiting for intruders. The imagination could run wild with such a subject. The artist can find extensive information relating to ships of various design, age, and origin by referring to historical journals and magazines. *National Geographic* often has articles of pertinent value in this respect. The subject is so broad that one need only secure specific information relating to an area and then let the ideas come. The process of gathering information and then applying imagination is a two-fold combination that can't be beat.

"Saint Peter Liberated by the Angel"
by Rembrandt Van Rijn
Courtesy, Crocker Art Gallery,
Sacramento, California

The artist is a perceiver who pays special attention to the points of view from which the world can be seen, and one who catches and records for the rest of us the most revealing perspective on things.[1]

Chapter 12

Getting Ideas
from Other Artists

This final chapter deals with artists — their art products, the art media they use, and the ideas that can be derived from a study of their work. To study the work of a specific artist, one should gather a representative sampling. The original works of well-known artists are usually not accessible except in limited quantities at the major galleries. Libraries, however, can bring many excellent reproductions into reach. Through books, the entire life work of an artist can be revealed to the searching student. The study of reproductions can be enriched by frequent trips to major galleries to study the originals. If nationally recognized works are not available, the products of younger artists can be examined. It is vital to aesthetic growth that the student of art observe all that is being done around him. One grows more soundly in his own art when he can share ideas, and discuss techniques and possibilities with fellow students. Inexperienced students will often work in styles that are currently popular or that follow closely the successful statements of a more mature artist in the community. This can be a sound approach, for working in a manner that has been tested by veterans is a way of learning the medium and understanding what another artist has done with it. It is only when the student *continues* to imitate the work of another that he fails to grow. Sooner or later, each student must release himself from the teachings of his masters and step into the art world on his own ground. He may ally himself with a group and work toward a common goal for art expression, but his work should remain his own.

Intensifying the Search for Ideas

Many times while examining the work of other artists, it may appear that we are not moved by the subject. Here is the time to remember that the intellect is similar to the operation of a camera. That is, the frames of the mind and the imagination keep clicking away, although verbal or aesthetic expression may seem distant. The seedlings of inspiration are being tucked away to wait for the catalyst that will release the power train. It might be two years or more before an experience that one has had will have practical application for aesthetic expression. Often, we incorporate ideas in our art work without realizing their sources of inspiration. They are part of the free flow of imaginative outpourings that all creative individuals have developed. It is often puzzling to the person not engaged in art processes that the artist is able to *dream up* so many ideas so often and so spontaneously. However, it is *not* a question of pulling rabbits from a magic hat. It is rather a question of developing the creative power that one has been granted at birth. The artist has done this by building up his ability to see the world *with sensitive feelers.* He has learned to experience life deeply *through the development of his awareness:* awareness *to ideas* and *to experiences,* and *self-awareness.*[2]

The beginning art student must ask himself many questions in relation to the work of others. Some of these include:

> *Why does the artist work this way?*
> *How does he use the art media?*
> *How has he composed the art work?*
> *Why did he choose this material?*
> *What makes the work an individual expression?*

These are questions that can only be answered in a personal way as a result of a visual and imaginative search.

Art History as an Idea Source

Studying the history of art can be valuable to the growth of one's artistic expression. Through their art works, the artists of the past can provide leads and suggestions much in the way that early scientists broke ground for those who followed. One should study the works of the Renaissance masters as well as those of the nineteenth and twentieth century to gain insights and ideas. While the ground rules for art may vary, and new techniques may suggest unusual flourishes, art remains what it has always been. Being able to put all of the pieces of art together from the cave paintings down to the latest experimentations is a way of bringing artistic thought into a wholeness that allows one a proper perspective in relation to his own position.

Art magazines and journals help us to keep abreast of what is currently going on in art as well as what has been accomplished in the past. Art critics can often provide us with aesthetic cues for they are able to put into words what an artist has stated visually. They are also able to evaluate the work from a distance and thus see it in a more objective manner.

---

[2]Linderman, Earl W., "Curriculum For Awareness", *Journal of Art Education,* June, 1964.

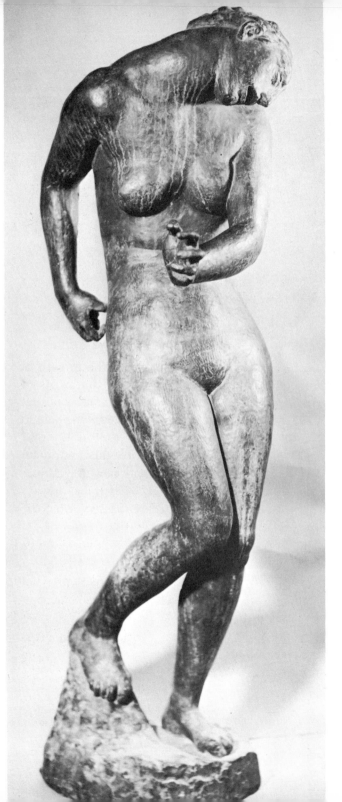

"Figure" by David Park
Courtesy, Crocker Art Gallery, Sacramento, California

"Atlantide" by Ivan Mestrovic
Courtesy, Crocker Art Gallery,
Sacramento, California

"Volcanic Pot" by Ted Wiprud
Courtesy of the artist

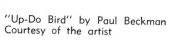

"Up-Do Bird" by Paul Beckman
Courtesy of the artist

Ceramic Jar by Marion Bowman
Courtesy of the artist

The Art Medium as a Source of Ideas

The art medium that one chooses to work with can often be a stimulating source of ideas. Some artists begin working in a medium without any particular idea or subject in mind. In sculpture, for example, an artist will often explore the materials by twisting, bending, piecing together, until he gets an inspiration that sends him in a particular direction. In this sense, the materials are the motivating factor. Many an artist will paint with his brush on canvas, creating form after form without prior intent. This process is not idle play, however. Much of creative expression is intuitive, and manipulating the medium is the artist's way of searching for cues that will suggest definite directions. At other times, the artist will approach his medium with a more definite idea in mind. His ideas may suggest the medium that he will use, so that there is always a fluid interaction between idea and material. Sometimes ideas suggest materials, and at other times materials suggest ideas. Often, visual information that can be useful to an artist can be obtained by studying works of art which relate to what one is doing at the present time. For example, if one were drawing with pen and ink, the thing to do would be to study everything available that had been done in pen and ink. This process would apply to any medium and any subject.

Taking a Critical Look at Our Own Art Works

Another means of determining growth in art is to examine and evaluate one's own work. After a time, it is necessary to step back and take a good hard look at what we have created. In this respect, it would be pertinent to date the work on the back and to keep at least one sample from each series so that accomplishments can be measured in terms of strengths and weaknesses. Evidence of growth is not always apparent in the product. And when it is observable in the work, it is not necessarily in a state that can be discussed verbally. Much of what is meaningful in art is intuitively expressed by the artist. It is a result of a flow of information that comes from deep within the person.

Where Some Artists Get Their Ideas for Their Art

It seems appropriate to conclude this visual adventure of ideas with a sampling of the work and statements of a number of professional artists. The selection is by no means all-inclusive or final. Rather, the statements and photographs which follow are intended as examples of the artistic point of view. The verbal message of each artist is intended to help clarify what he has expressed in visual terms. These statements, in both visual and verbal media show the great variation in personal expression. No artist is like any other artist — each emphasizes the individual nature of man and his ideas. The art product then is the sum total of a search; an expression in visual terms of what one has experienced and felt and thought. As such it represents the last stage of a continuing process. It is a stopping point for a *particular* search. New ideas, new inventions, and new sources for ideas and aesthetic evolutions will set the stage for future statements in art media. The end, or art statement contains the seedlings of new beginnings.

"Abstraction Based on Medieval Archetypes" by Howard Conant
50 x 118", enamel, tissue, and acrylic on canvas, 1965.
Courtesy of the artist

My fundamental concepts for this work sprang from my continuing interest in medieval art forms, and in lettering, particularly in the letter forms of "U" and "A," etc. I look at these forms and am inspired by them, and base my work upon their appearances and my reactions to them. I begin working on such works (this one is 118″ wide) by sketching certain shapes in charcoal, modifying them, and then painting them with oil, enamel, glued tissue, and photographic tape, sometimes with acrylic paint, and then by making subsequent revisions based on the formal relationships of the shapes I've created. Each work takes me about two years, during which time I look at them and revise them often, and also start new works. My main interest in this and other works is to achieve the highest possible level of aesthetic significance through composition (mainly), color, and shape relationships.

HOWARD CONANT

Without planning consciously, I came up with the composition which became the birds on the beach called finally "Beach Genre." This lithograph came about in the following manner: I was idly playing with a pencil and unthinkingly jotted down some scattered black spots. Over these I drew some dark vertical lines. When these two image dispersions overlapped I recalled vividly an experience some few days earlier, when walking at the ocean during grey weather I had seen scores of small sandpipers busily searching food among beach grass clumps. Their detached intensity, their blackness, their group efforts, and the partial hidden curtain afforded by the bending grasses in the grey wetness of Oregon's winter came alive again in the very crude and almost meaningless sketch. From that I drew the lithograph. Although as I worked I altered scale and made my birds to my own desires.

NELSON SANDGREN

"Beach Genre" by Nelson Sandgren

Painting by Ralph L. Goings
Courtesy, Crocker Art Gallery, Sacramento, California

My painting stems from a need to make images for I believe the image is the most important aspect of painting. I have no interest in the niceties of "formal composition"; the rectangle of the canvas is simply the support for the painted image. I am interested in the visual and intellectual relationships between the various images that I use. I try to make them visually sensual and intellectually provocative. These relationships have an accidental quality at times because I often choose images at random to combine in the same painting. However, my greatest concern is for the careful rendering of the image.

Magazine photographs provide the working stimulus for me. I have a large collection which I enjoy looking through. As I run across images that interest me I pin them to my studio walls which are always covered with photographs. From the wall some of these images, one way or another, find their way into my paintings. I have no set way of beginning a painting; sometimes a whole set of images will fall together, and the painting will be conceived at one time. At other times I begin with one image and add others as the painting progresses. In either case each image is painted completely in one sitting while the paint is wet and plastic. It must be right the first time. I seldom place forms in an environment because it detracts from the clarity of the image. This also eliminates the necessity for creating logical space relationships. The implied space surrounding realistic images becomes more dynamic when it doesn't have to conform to any kind of regimen.

RALPH L. GOINGS

"Predator" by Bruce Carter
Photograph by Angela Zelver

"Hear me, predator! We have seen the handi-work of your warped, sick mind in the bloodied backs and stretched necks of lynched Negro tobacco pickers, in the resigned conviction of a Jewish father and his young son, standing naked, holding hands, awaiting their turn in your lime pits. We have seen your barbarity, vividly displayed in Goya's "Disasters of War" and Callot's "Miseries of War." We have read of your senseless savagery in the records of the Spanish Conquistadors in Mexico and Peru.

Wounded Knee, Andersonville, Bergen, Belsen, Cholula, Televaag, and Lidice.

We stand bewildered and wonder why such a beast as you is included in the roll call of human beings. We are choked with angry frustration as we try to explain to our sons the futility of your heinous deeds."

BRUCE CARTER

I get my ideas from reading and reacting to and with other human beings daily. I'm a perceptual "blotter." In terms of beginning my work, I carry many impressions in my mind for sometimes weeks, and then a fusion of these fragments occurs, and a personal image begins to suggest the intensity of my reactions and the complexity of its meanings. I draw these images sometimes with a felt marker or directly with the knife on the block and begin to cut until I am completed with the block, then proof it, etc. I often hang a proof in my studio for several weeks to allow my rather prejudiced reaction a time to stabilize and become more objective. Sometimes this has lead to sawing blocks into three or four separate pieces and reassembling. Other times color has been the necessary additive. My colleagues are merciless with their criticism, and I listen and learn.

BRUCE CARTER

"Elisha" by Don Uhlin
Photograph by Ralph Talbert

The print titled *Elisha* is typical of my intaglio work and indicates the personal interaction I have with the materials. In the print process I find that the materials tend to control expression by the nature of their characteristics, and this is very frustrating to the beginner. The experienced printmaker allows the materials to speak to him and by responding to them, rather than attempting to subordinate them to his control, he finds them to stimulate much of the basic print quality. It is a sensitivity then which must be developed for material and process that I find to be imperative in my printmaking. In this print I turned the entire plate black with aquatint in order to work from black to white values. As I started scraping, the whiteness of the metal suggested the bald, shiny head of Elisha (II Kings 2:23-24) and thus the subject of the print was established. It should be mentioned that much of my work is established upon Biblical reference though the subject is in all cases integrated with process and the quality of the work is not subordinated to a visual and literal interpretation found commonly in illustration. The scraping and burnishing of the copper from a black aquatint surface produced not only a soft edge to tonal areas but it also enabled high contrast with rich texture.

Don Uhlin

I start with drawings, nothing fancy, just something to visualize my ideas, what I'm saying and how I'm going to say it. These are not working drawings, just papers that keep me thinking. I'll decide on the medium. I prefer clay because it's open to all plastic suggestions; but, if the idea is better suited to metal casting, then I'll work in micro-crystalline wax. Complete knowledge of the medium is essential, since technical hang-ups can nullify the concept. Once working in the medium, I discard the drawings. Occasionally, I will make new drawings from a half-completed sculpture to work out alternatives. Usually, though, these alternatives take the form of additional sculptures as variations on a theme. When I'm working in clay, I often use the potter's wheel as a tool for rapid forming of basic volumes. I use a coarse clay with 30% gray. If the piece is going to be quite large, I'll work it in sections to be epoxyed together after firing. I usually incorporate poly-chrome glazes in my ceramic sculpture form. If I'm working in wax for a metal casting, I usually try to incorporate a ready made object which further develops the concept, such as my series of bronze figures with cast corsets.

ROBERT ARNESON

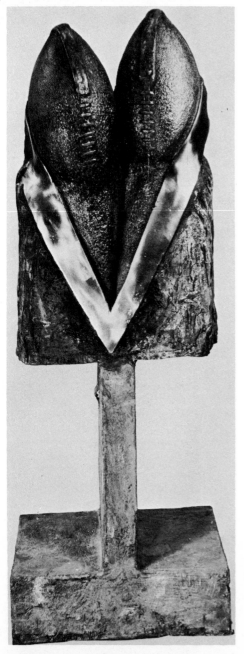

"Football Queen" by Robert Arneson
Courtesy of the artist

"Mother Bird" by Robert Arneson
Courtesy of the artist

My hangings are conceived as decorative statements in cloth, influenced by traditional qualities of craftsmanship as well as the compelling, challenging images of contemporary art. The themes are derived from personal environments: beach, common objects, mountains. The perpetual movement of the sea and the spacial relationships of sand, water, rocks, grass, mountains, and valleys lend themselves to decorative patterns. Some hangings develop from sketches while others are inspired only by the compositional manipulations of the fabrics. My more recent hangings relate to assemblage and make use of cloth-found objects. In these, an effort has been made to work directly with my own environment through the integration of these extraneous materials into the work of art. These experimental hangings indicate many exciting new directions in this area that I am currently investigating.

MARILYN PAPPAS

"Shirt" by Marilyn Pappas
Courtesy of the artist

"Interior" by Alan Munro
Photograph by Angela Zelver

I remember the shapes of trees, faces, mountain masses and the intricacies of night neons. I remember the timeless tides of Oregon beaches and sunbathing youths. The plants of our garden inspire me to make painted areas of intense color, complex texture, green lines shaped by the actions of growth. My opinions of current happenings or even disasters of a political, social or moral nature are subjects for my paintings at times. To the watercolor paper or oil painting surface I bring a storehouse of personal visual experience. Any one subject interest of the artist can be said more than one way. I find that I feel compelled to invent more than one way to say it in order to feel satisfied that I have stated it to the best of my ability. As I change with time and maturity I return to ideas that I have painted years ago to bring them to a higher resolve.

Art is the history of man's ideas made visible. My ideas concerning the divine, nature, the man-made and man himself within this age are important sources for my art. To change a mental image into a visual image I freely experiment with the inside of the idea as well as the outside. Experimentation is done with my materials, also. To make new visual discoveries enables me to express my ideas, opinions and personal experiences in a direct, ordered, visual statement.

ALAN MUNRO

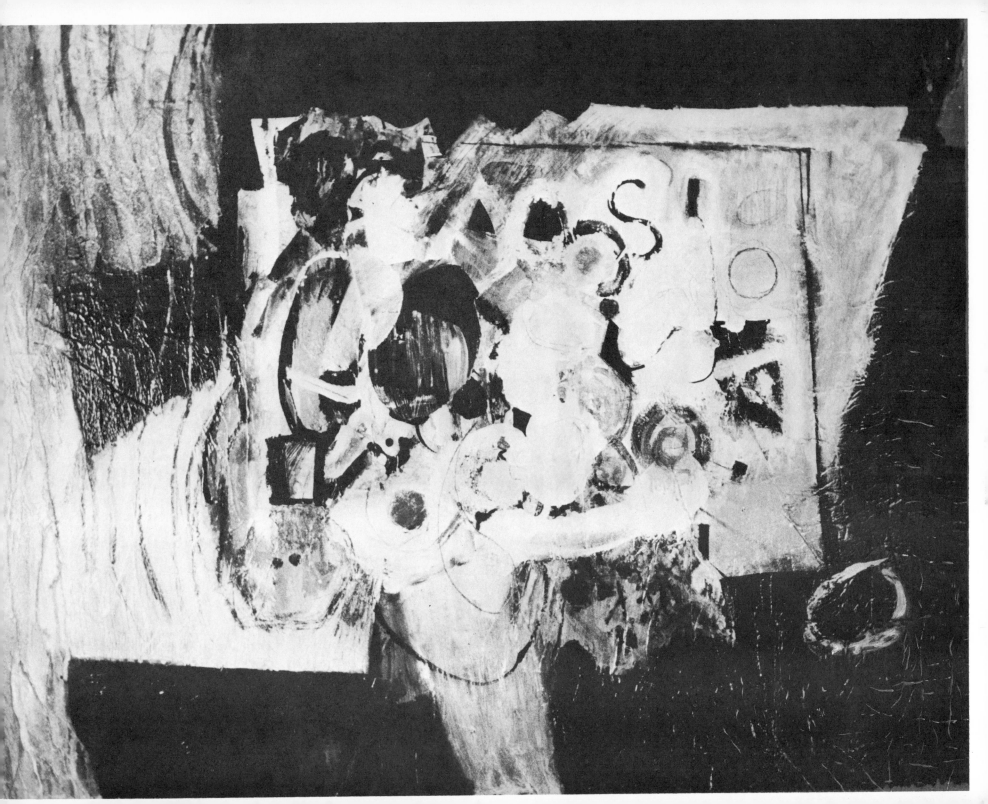

"Glory Forbes - Vigilante" by Mel Ramos
Courtesy, Bianchini Birillo Gallery, New York

My ideas come from a very obvious source: middle-class consciousness. They have come from a very gradual process of personal involvement with "dada," American landscapes and submerged sexual connotations inherent in mass advertising. The idea of sex in advertising which appeals to the middle class sensibility, but which is watered down to satisfy a self-imposed moral code, has always fascinated me. "Madison Avenue" taste-makers often appeal indirectly to our subconscious erotic desires. I do not reject this idea; quite the contrary, my work is an affirmation of this concept. The incongruity of a beautiful, young, sexy, sensuous "girlie" and a cold, hard, impersonal, banal object (i.e. spark plug) seems such a perfect relationship; a match made in heaven. Americans are hero-worshippers and I think of myself as an iconographer.

I usually begin my work, after having considered the possible combinations I will use, by gathering several photographs of objects from popular magazines like Life, Look, Motor Trend, Time, Vogue, etc.; and also from the "girlie" magazines like Playboy, Cavalier, Escapade, etc. I select photos that will work together and use them to make a working drawing from. When the drawing is right I blow it up on the canvas and paint it as directly as I possibly can without becoming too romantic about the subject. This often does not work for me as the paintings are more often than not, very romantic. However, this is not a big point with me and I do not have anything against romanticism.

MEL RAMOS

I find it helpful to begin my work with a visual subject before me. One must also acquaint himself with the materials being used. If I decide to draw with ink, brush and pen, I must experiment and draw over and over again, always trying many different ways to work with the material until the most satisfying approaches and ideas begin to come. As I paint, and the more I paint, I find different things will happen with the surface — exciting things. If I could predict how the material were to respond each time I used the paint, I would find painting very dull. The pleasure, the delight in constantly discovering new solutions and combinations to titilate the eyes — these are the rewards of the challenge of paint, or of art.

My subject is often a model. After working with the material and the subject for many months, I begin to feel results that are satisfying to myself. To me, it is important to capture the essence of the subject by interpreting it through my own experience with it. It is always a question of what to include, what to omit — how simply can I keep the forms before I lose the entity? Tomorrow it will be different.

MARLENE LINDERMAN

"After Dinner" by Marlene Linderman

I am a formalist. Art is not easy or fun at times like some say. It is plain hard work. I look at it as "life" in its full strength whether I am aware of humans or unaware of their existence in my work. Though living in a large city, I am not aware in my paintings of its crowded conditions.

I rarely paint *from* nature. I rely on my expressing a thought which has been formulated by the constant close observance of nature and through photography. I generally tend to reorganize my thoughts. Therefore, I simplify nature like peeling an onion, one skin at a time. Then when I am satisfied with the structure I rely on my skills to carry it from there. I am constantly aware of the masters. This helps me in strengthening certain convictions in painting. At times, I discipline myself with hard rendering, and drawing the model. This close awareness makes me more critical of my thoughts.

I generally use a horizontal format. My media is generally thick and worked fluidly. I rely a great deal on the paint being just right in areas so that my thoughts can take hold. The brush stroke is generally one of speed or one that tails off into silence. Shapes take place in the distance in most of my paintings because I like to be aware of the big earth in its relationship to the universe. I am also aware of the importance of a thin hair-line in painting with the contrast of a wide brush stroke. I dominate my paintings with blue and white. My paintings seem to work with this color choice. I am a representational painter but not realistic. Identity is immediately grasped by the viewers. Light and air is my primary concern along with sound structure.

GREGORY KONDOS

"Ekonostasi" by Gregory Kondos
Courtesy of the artist

Woodprint by Paul Gunn
Photograph by Angela Zelver

Ideas for my paintings come from a variety of sources, some of which I can understand and describe. One method of working is to develop a landscape idea from a natural scrap, i.e., a seascape from the surface pattern on a snail shell, a forest theme from the pattern on a piece of bark. I think there is some validity in the process of examining nature's productions on a two-dimensional surface as a starting point for a two-dimensional work, even though the work does, in its finished state, deal with the illusion of space.

To begin a painting, I lay the panel on the floor and pour dirty turpentine on it. I cannot face an empty surface. Something must be there in the beginning for me to become involved with. Many of my woodcuts are begun by printing the solid, uncarved surface of a piece of wood. The nature of that piece of wood can generate, or at least direct, the nature of the finished print.

PAUL GUNN

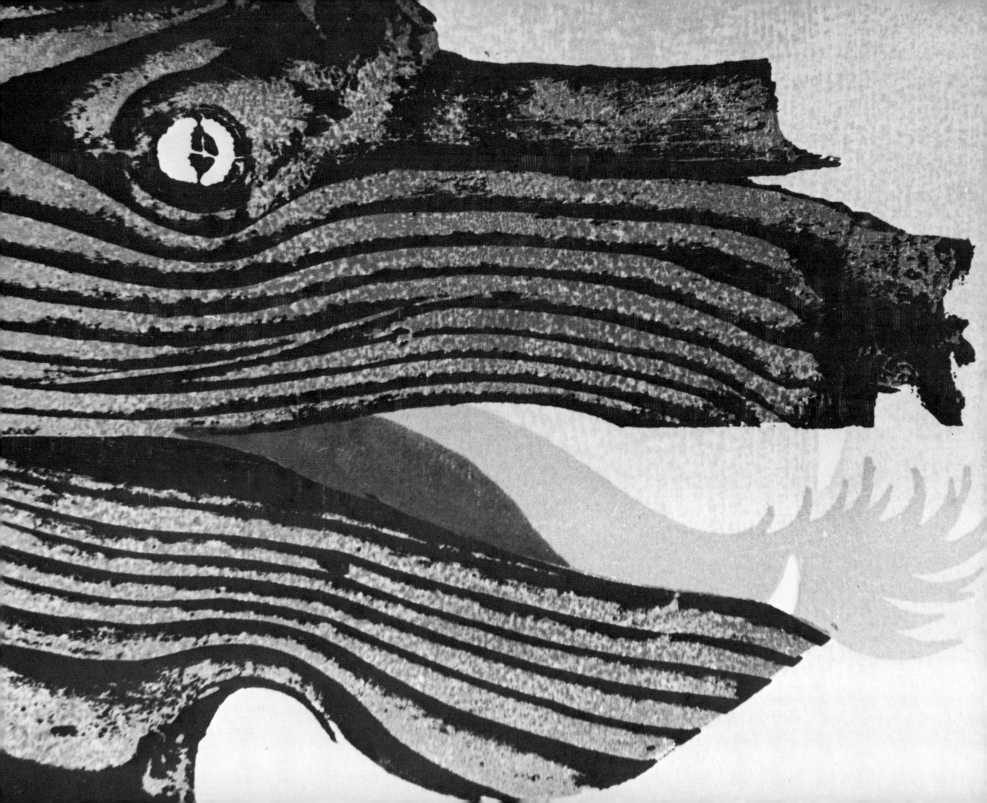

Ideas for my optical art paintings are readily available. The field of visual illusion has been extensively investigated and examples of design based on mathematical progressions and optical effects are plentiful. Scientific and mathematical publications are excellent sources for such designs. I usually start with one of these ideas and try to add something new or unusual as the painting progresses. I like to use optical illusions and vibrating colors but feel that some relief should be introduced so that the painting is not visually repellent to the observer. The use of textural areas or areas of quiet color with the optical devices produces a type of optical hard-edge abstract art which I feel has a great deal of interest. I believe that op art's dynamic and forceful impact will have a pronounced effect on some future development in art.

WILLIAM C. MACARTHUR

"Carnival" by William C. MacArthur
Courtesy of the artist

"Lipstick Rows" by Wayne Thiebaud
Courtesy of the artist

Painting by Wayne Thiebaud
Courtesy, Crocker Art Gallery, Sacramento, California

For the past three years I have been working directly from the figure. Differences between a glance and a stare fascinate me. Staring at something that stares back does something to the visual field. The moment seems expanded and clarified by focus and engagement. Staring at an individual directly across from you in a well-lighted white-walled room gives you a great deal of information about his physical existence. Because we know nothing about the inside of this same person we use the seeable things like rings, shoes, watches, badges, buttons, style and manner to suggest possibilities for fascinating speculation.

The propensities of oil paint to suggest variable kinds of subject matter makes it my present medium. Its capacities are somehow more related to skin, oil and other substances in our bodies. The sticky, shiny effects are very necessary for my present work. I use standard oil colors in tubes, and I thin or extend them with a mixture of one-third stand oil or damar varnish, one-third linseed oil and one-third turpentine.

After a pose is decided upon I begin to draw upon the primed canvas with a bristle brush and diluted lemon yellow paint. After this initial over-all drawing I make another drawing in a different color. I try to draw the entire thing each time, and to make corrections and changes as I go along. As many as eight to twelve drawings of this kind are made in as many colors, i.e. golden yellow, cadmium red, alizarin crimson, cerulean blue, ultramarine blue, lime green, rose pink, and others. When this is well along I start to paint, allowing some of these original drawing lines to remain and become part of the final painting.

WAYNE THIEBAUD

For me a work of art is a document of the personality of the artist: his soul, sensitivity, and his temperament. It is a constant search for his own true self. It becomes his way of life, his document of the century in which he lives. For example, when I wander off across rocks, cliffs, and soft sands, under a dome of evergreens into brittle craters of color, or across town into avenues of brick and glass with the multitudes, I observe and respond to this world about me as a child, with simple and spontaneous joy. I can then seize an instant from this experience and imprison it by means of ordered shapes, color, form, pattern, space and time relationships.

I am not seeking pure abstraction but rather the purity and essence of the idea expressed in simple form. My canvas then becomes the arena in which I do battle; it becomes a recording, or a situation in nature where I try to create an equilibrium between the basic factors of painting, meaning and image, in such a way that these factors are inspired by past and present experiences, by the impressions of life that have been etched upon my mind and expressed in terms of paint forming a picture.

DEMETRIOS JAMESON

"The Widows" by Demetrios Jameson
Courtesy of the artist

I know it will sound arbitrary and self-centered, but to a large degree I get my ideas from my own perception. By this I mean something really quite simple but not at all obvious to an onlooker. From my youngest conscious memories, I recall the feeling of the difference between the way things "are" (or are said to be), the way they are to me at any moment, and the way they change when I move toward them — through mind, feelings, and medium. Sensed in this way, everything is really quite a convention from the one side and quite, even hopelessly, idiosyncratic, from the other. In this feeling, the child, man and artist in me are all one.

Secondly, there are perennial themes behind my images. The "river," is such a one for me. It is not the "real" Susquehanna which I walked along daily for several decades, but a deeper residual of layer after layer of its lights, its distances, and the vistas through which it is approached. Another theme is more or less a gothic kind of aspiration. I used to see it in nature, but now that I no longer make any simple translation from nature into art, I see it in my pots, which thrust upward through distortion, exaggeration, and even clumsiness. Tall necks, exaggerated lips, and narrow cylindrical bodies come from this source in my pottery, as does also a certain ceremonial air. Both themes mentioned also connect to my childhood spent in church, as a preacher's son, and from the fact that my worlds always merge in my images, no matter how discontinuous they may seem in my daily schedule. Add to these my long standing love for the polyphonic and contrapuntal music of Bach and you have some idea of the cementing agent of my inner vision.

Finally, the full circle to simplicity, trust, and primitivity occurs in my love for "goonies." These are literally man-made stones — stoneware stones, which I throw on the wheel into round and completely closed shapes, then paddle, when leather hard, with simple inlays of dark clay. The light lines are cut from the areas where I lay on no-black engobe and are set into cut out grooves in the black areas, and vice versa. Then I paddle again and so on. The method allows only directness and then further transforms that directness.

Lastly, all things relate. Paintings and drawings influence pots and vice versa. The river shows up on a sgraffito pot and "gooney-scratches" show up in drawings. So the final and continuing source of ideas is really from one object to the next. I love to go through thematic variation as long as a vein does not run out. And when they seem to have run out, I am patient: I find they have only gone underground. Then my mortality, the continuity of all things, and the continuing miracle of consciousness strike me dumb with terror, awe, resignation, and humility — but always lead to a new act, a new work. What else it means, I don't know and don't care.

Literally, I just begin — sometimes where I left off previously, but often anywhere at all that seems important at the time. Like a good discussion, I envision the working process as a dialogue, which means to me that I and the topic and the medium will be further revealed transactionally. The irreversible and unpredictable are inevitable anyway, so they might as well be counted. Thus I include repetition (of previous ideas, as in a brushing theme for a pot, for I know it will always be different), chance or serendipity, and, especially, "feedback" from first act, stroke, or form to the next. Free association is always there, and odd combinations of ideas and operations in the medium swell and sink like some natural phenomenon. I am no more in control than I am out of control. I am "responsible" but always surprised or seeking surprise.

On a deeper level, the whole process is at times a trance-like immersion out of time. Ideas and images may well up from semi-dream states of the night before, or I may set myself thinking of a topic, such as a grouping of goonies, and end up sensing them snuggled together in a cluster in a bigger "half-gooney" like peas in a pod, or pressing against one another and flattening each other, like bubbles in a froth-structure. Again, a single, large shape may present itself to me.

But my way of working is usually off-center. I have only to begin, then choose, then reflect and choose again, and I am off in a new chain of associations and operations (medium transformations). Thus I usually don't strive to be original or novel. That is a natural consequence of dialogue, of life. As in the statement of Buber's about dialogue, there is nothing I have that I feel is irrelevant and there is nothing I don't have that is relevant to this dialogue — now! I am not talking of "success," but what counts from my side of the affair.

KENNETH R. BEITTEL

Ceramic Ware by Kenneth R. Beittel

"Natureform" by Anna Ballarian
Courtesy of the artist

Nature is the main source of inspiration that sets off the spark for my artistic creations. Even though I believe that the outward appearance of nature is but the shell for a deeper richer world which I am curious to discover, and understand; intuitively relating shapes, colors, textures, materials in inventive ways is most satisfying. I like to have first hand experiences — to work directly with the forms from nature, to observe them from various points of view. While the best sketch book is in the eye, I am constantly drawing and observing flowers in the sunlight, in the breeze, in order to capture the spirit of my environment. In my travels to new and strange places, I fill many sketch books. One day, for instance, I sketched for hours in a friend's rock garden. I could have photographed much more accurately, but to make my own symbols of line, shape, and colors can capture the spirit more expressively of what I feel. No matter what medium I use, I like to work directly in it whether it be cloth, stones, or paint. I enjoy especially to work with mixed media, because I like the unique qualities of textures and colors achieved to get the total desired effects in the work of art.

ANNA BALLARIAN

"The Conductor" by Shepard Levine
Courtesy of the artist

An idea is a cumulative development. It is both sequential and experiential. It is not one or two isolated events, but it exists in a continuum, much the same way humans live. There are certain strands of these experiences for which personal affinities are developed, and these constitute the grist mill for thematic material — but this has not to do with subject matter as much as the relationship to it. This introduces the nature of value systems — how and why we select. There is a mystique to this process, and so the assumption must be made that we can never fully fathom the process intellectually. However, we can and must appreciate that art grows out of art and that this regenerative force is essential to an intelligent and sensitive process of immersion — a continual baptism of the "art-idea."

There is a condition of work which must prevail in the development of ideas. An idea must be isolated and examined, it must be synthesized, tried, and if necessary, thrown out. One hopefully begins where one has left off, stimulated into moving vertically as well as horizontally; to new relationships, refreshed approaches, to areas of invention rather than innovation. The ultimate creative despair is to "plateau out," the ultimate joy, to grab for and succeed in reaching a new and further horizon — and to keep on doing this.

SHEPARD LEVINE

Pottery isn't what's important for me — it's the clay — it's immediate; you push it, pull it, carve it, press it and it retains the image — it is very closely associated with "action painting" (Pollock, Kline, etc.). A potter isn't a guy that makes items — or ware. A potter puts life into his material. We can all make a bowl, a cup, a pot, but it is a greater feat to create a form that has part of you in it — your feelings, ideas, shapes, fingerprints. Sometimes when I finish a pot, I chuckle, laugh or just look at it — as if I don't know it, as if there are parts of myself I still do not know; but the pot has a life.

A potter must experiment with his clay — his form — pushing them to their extremes to see when the clay breaks and collapses and then, where does he fit in? Sometimes I add clay forms, paint them, squeeze them — but most important it is an amalgamation of clay and artist into one thing. I believe in making my pieces in one sitting if possible. That is, constructing, throwing, and decorating all at once; even decorating before all the pieces have been added. This way I can complete the pot while I am still thinking about it. As I am concerned with hard edges, black against white, soft against crisp, and brighter colors, I find that my methods of decoration become most important and I have all but forgotten the aspects of throwing. Sometimes plates are made with *one pull* and then altered, pinched and painted. Sometimes forms are made and painted entirely white, or all black — completely covering all the clay characteristics as such but emphasizing the form, the crisp shapes. Although these pots have been my latest efforts they are the least appreciated by others. People laugh and say I ought to stick to my old pots; I get rejected from shows (four in a row). But to me they have merit. They are what I am at the time, what I want to make. So I keep on making them — I like them.

BILL FARRELL

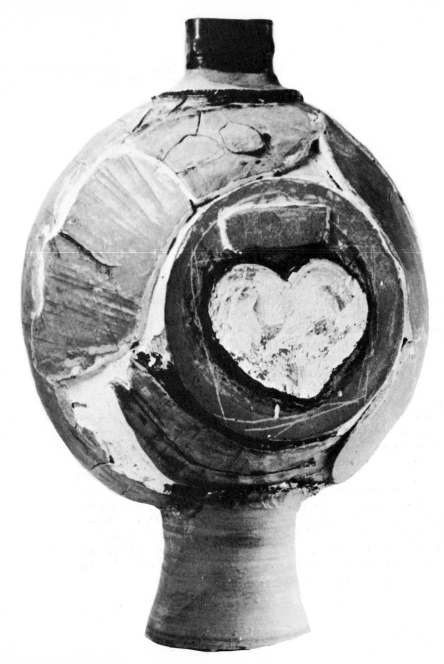

"My Favorite Flower" by Bill Farrell
Courtesy of the artist

The question of the origin of an idea in a work of art is a baffling one. In asking this question of those of us who practice the witchcraft called art, one will get as many answers as there are artists. My particular answer is a simple one — from people and the things they do (and in some cases, things they *don't* do). I have many times been accused of being too literary in my work and perhaps that is true. But then I have found that the verbal imagery as used by poets is no less intriguing when it is transposed into the visual.

I would say then that life itself as lived by us all — the beautiful ones, the ugly ones, the good ones, the vicious ones — is the birthplace of my "ideas" for I believe that an art divorced from the human element is an art somehow lacking in force. And if that "life" is from a poem, a story, or even that place we call "reality," then it really doesn't matter for the line drawn between the real and the unreal becomes somehow unimportant in the work of art.

As for how it all begins on the canvas, that is an easy question to answer. For me it begins with drawing of the image with the particular quality of the line being suited to what is being drawn. From there it is a simple matter of color and light.

BERK CHAPPELL

"Ready for the Reliquary" by Berk Chappell
Courtesy of the artist

"Slow Burn," (Intaglio) by Gordon W. Gilkey

My prints grow from visual image stimulations (my visual environment) or, as is more often the case, from thoughts seeking visual expression. In either event, the thought, the visual stimulation, or combinations of both, become the starting point for the work.

I do not make detailed advance drawings which would then become inhibited, rendered translations of such drawings into etched copper printing plates. Rather, the work grows and develops on and then into the copper. Here the creative decisions are made. A certain desired spontaneity thus results and the printed proof records, in a more intimate way, the creative decisions which produced the work. I avoid calling the "work" an "art work." Whether or not the final proofs are successful . . . that is for others to decide. The prints must be more than mere technical exercises. I make use of the technical tools and processes as a means of expression and not as an end. Virtuosity I can admire in others.

As to my finished prints, I am prepared to discuss with fellow printmakers the mixture of acids and inks, the merits of various papers and presses. I discuss with collectors curatorial problems and to others I often give advice about mats and frames. But I do not comment about specific prints. They are my children and they will stand or fall on their own merits. They have their own lives to live. I do wish them well.

GORDON GILKEY

I use whatever sources are available to get ideas for my art. To be more explicit, the world of nature and man are inexhaustible sources of inspiration for the artist. As I think about what I want to say in my work, two different aspects of life are generally reflected — the conscious and the unconscious. When I'm seeking ideas of a conscious nature I have only to scan through sketches of previous visual experiences and re-record them with paint and brush. The idea at this time is reborn and takes on new meaning and feeling as the shapes and composition evolve in the finished work. Perhaps my most urgent need for self expression falls in the category of the unconscious, semi-conscious, or psychological aspects of life. Actually, some may interpret this to mean non-objective surrealist, or even abstract painting. It's not unusual for me to lay half-asleep and begin to conjure up ideas about a painting I have not yet done, but then immediately file it mentally for future reference. Upon closing my eyes, new shapes, images, and colors may begin to take over and ultimately result in an idea for a new painting. Naturally, the finished painting may reflect or contain specific abstract or semi-abstract shapes or images of conscious visual experiences of the past or present.

Once I think that I have an idea that can be developed, I immediately begin to put it down with quick black and white pencil or charcoal sketches. I'm a firm believer in the thumbnail sketch as a means of spontaneous development of the idea. Following a series of such sketches and eventual selection of the best, I then attempt to develop the sketch into a finished composition. I have never dwelled on the need for color sketches, but rather find the depth and values of light and dark contrasts more than adequate for completion of the final work. The eventual development of the work in the chosen medium begins to take place after this procedure has been followed.

WILLIAM J. KASZA

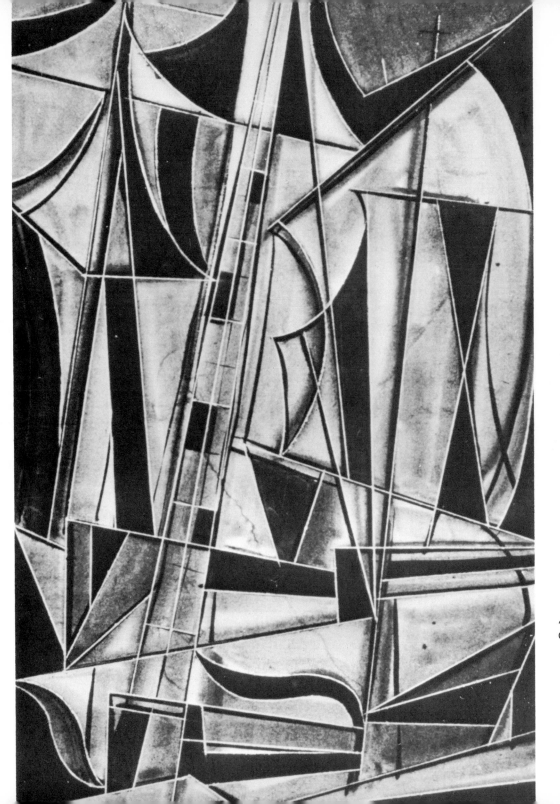

"Balboa" by William J. Kasza
Courtesy of the artist

My ideas come mainly from two rather direct sources. The first, and most immediate source is nature. Perhaps a better term would be "life" as it affects, and is effected by nature. At one time my best ideas seemed to come to me at isolated moments and in out-of-the-ordinary situations and my greatest concern was that those ideas would be lost or lose their impact if I didn't react quickly. Now I am beginning to realize that the best ideas have a lingering quality that improves with time. For example, a new or different idea may appear to me from my environment, generally as a development of earlier ideas, and I attempt to "toy" with it as long as possible. This, I feel allows both the idea and my relationship to it, to develop to the fullest before I take any action. Sometimes the idea must be entertained in a real way, through a series of paintings, but other times it is but a mental manipulation of possibilities. I consciously try to exhaust the idea, exploiting it in various ways, even ignoring it or reversing tack until I feel that it can begin to stand by itself.

Once the idea has proven sound, the task of bringing it to a life of its own is begun. This brings me to the second source of ideas as well as the supplemental stuff of beginning a work. I rely on and am greatly influenced by the arts of yesterday. By that I mean that I draw on ideas of others; ideas which have already gone through serious evaluation processes and which have stood the test of time, whether a moment or a century. Adolph Gotlieb and Josef Albers both have influenced my general direction in terms of icon with the former, and color with the latter.

The actual beginning of a new work is the most difficult and soul rending act I know of. Facing a pure panel with a new idea takes colossal nerve and not until the first stroke of form is put down, do I relate to the goodness of the idea itself. Once that first statement is made the work seems to flow until that final act is necessary . . . stopping. Many times I've found that I have stopped too early and have gone back into the painting as much as a year later to complete it.

I work only with polymer pigments now, being more flexible for my needs over oils. I also make use of fabrics and other materials, in order to complete an idea, through a collage technique. In the beginning, I usually work for a time with the under colors, which will become a statement of ground for the idea or figure. This phase is generally rather open and experimental and will undergo many changes before the central idea is permitted to emerge. After laying in areas I will often combine fabrics and other materials within areas of color in order to lift the surface in terms of three dimensional form. Then, thin layers of color are laid over the raised surfaces creating peaks and valleys of interest as well as justifying whatever form may be emerging. It is a matter of working with the whole through each contributing part, waiting and watching as each mark alters the last and predicts the next.

HERBERT J. BURGART

Courtesy by Herbert J. Burgart

If I knew where good ideas come from, I would move there. For me the most difficult phase of the creative act is the initiation of a *really good idea*. Invariably, I must start with something that does not satisfy me, with the hope that I can make it into something better. I am generally annoyed with my beginning design and never satisfied with my craftsmanship. I realize that I have spent far too few hours developing my skills. I begin with an incomplete sketch. On the rug illustrated, I began with a simple "sun" shape on a rectangular background. I use the "sun" shapes frequently, but for no conscious reason. My initial intent in this instance was to use two basic shapes, the circle and rectangle, to develop a simple relationship. I wanted to create a rather baroque or rococo "business" around the circle to disturb the tranquility of the original relationship. I tried to have everything radiate from the sun center. Other than these few decisions, I decided to "play it by ear" as I hooked. My method of hooking allows me to work with only about a sixth of the rug at a time, the other five-sixths is hidden. Working spontaneously to elaborate the design and to develop necessary textures which the design seems to call forth is apt to create many surprises — not all of them happy ones. Usually, I end up somewhat better than I started but rarely with a feeling of being fully satisfied.

"Orbiting Space Junk" by Polly Mattil and Edward Mattil Hooked Wool Rug, 48 x 108"

The act of creating provides neither joy or "fun" for me. I struggle endlessly for an initial idea, which most often is unsatisfactory and frequently impossible. Sometimes I can't free myself from the first idea. It must be that my capacity for ideas is limited. I am always reflecting myself against the performances of full-time, life-time craftsmen and, of course, am embarrassed by my own inadequacies. Nevertheless, my urge to create is sufficient that I continue to move through these rather frustrating stages toward the finished object — be it a rug or a ring. I like the experience of the idea evolving as a result of the materials, the techniques I employ with tools and materials and the hope that the basic ideas may be transformed. I don't care about failure outside of my own feelings for I am not committed to show anybody anything, nor am I dependent upon approval through the sale of my products. My greatest weakness seems obvious to me — I lack the fluency necessary to generate loads of initial ideas from which to critically select the best ones for development. I don't mind melting down my jewelry and reusing the precious metals, but I'm too puritanical (or too Scotch) to destroy my rugs so they end up in use regardless of my final feeling. Incidentally, my rugs improve with a little dirt.

EDWARD L. MATTIL

I can only guess at some of the many ways ideas are triggered into the conscious mind from many internal and external stimuli. To be more specific, the following are some examples that I have attempted to trace back in my memory: the first source is through the material which I have collected and have in my studio, (The material may not bring forth an idea for as long as a year or two). The second source is through mistakes which I have made while working on a particular piece which may suggest the next half-dozen ideas. Third, looking through my collection of colored slides of details and close-ups of objects in nature often proves stimulating — this has become my way of "sketching." Fourth, looking at black and white photographs of my own work seems to be a way of retrieving lost ideas and of critically evaluating my sculpture. Fifth, when I accept a commission to do a creative piece, I am *forced* to expand my particular way of thinking and I personally find the demands and restrictions placed on the piece a really stimulating challenge that produces many new ideas.

I have no set way to begin work. Sometimes I start by cleaning up my work area of tools, scraps of metal, welding rods, and unfinished pieces of sculpture. At other times I start directly on the sculpture without delay. My approach depends on several factors, such as: how long it has been since I last took up my torch, how well thought out the idea is, whether I have made several sketches on paper, whether I have made a scale model in metal, and how secure I feel personally that day. Of late I have found that the cleaning of the studio releases me from the workaday world and outside distractions. I guess I have also reached the point where I wear certain shoes, pants, and shirt to set the attitude and mood for my personal release of creative thoughts from my subconscious.

DON HERBERHOLZ

"Day and Night," by Don Herberholz
Photograph by Barbara Herberholz

Transparent watercolor painting has always been fascinating to me and over a period of years I have worked and experimented continually with the medium. I have also felt a strong identity with oriental art and this seems to have complemented my love for nature.

Currently, I begin all paintings in a bathtub, large sink, or in an open stream. Using various sizes of pebble-mat board, I soak the surfaces for about 60 seconds and then I apply color into this saturated surface with a variety of brushes. All color areas are manipulated very broadly and without any subject matter reference. I generally work ten to fifteen boards at a time and over a period of a week or so I study the results. During this observation period I view them from all sides and generally pick one or two of the boards which have the most interesting configurations. I then start painting and base my treatment of subject matter to the potentialities of existing color areas. Sometimes, only one small area will give me an idea. The painting develops from general to specific shapes and I use all brushes in a calligraphic manner. Using this technique, I have painted watercolors from 12″ to 6′ in length. In the beginning, I have often found it convenient to cut my boards to the size of existing picture frames.

JAMES DOERTER

"Landscape" by James Doerter
Courtesy of the artist

Slab Bottle by Carl Cassady
Courtesy of the artist

It is hard to trace the origin of my ideas directly. It seems that the most profound ideas come through working and involvement. By working out one idea, tangent ideas and problems evolve. The more I work in clay, the more articulate I become. However, articulation is not enough. If this was the potter's only purpose he would display nothing but cold virtuosity. One must have something to say and know how to say it. I think the two should develop simultaneously. As the facility develops, so should awareness. Awareness is also stimulated by being cognizant of contributions to the field of ceramics through shows, magazines, and books. I find that I am influenced to a more or less degree by things that are going on in the art world today.

Since my approach to potting varies, sometimes drawings or studies precede the actual work and at other times the work is done directly. Some of the enjoyment of clay is lost when too much concern is given to a preconceived idea. That is to say, if the idea is well formed in mind or on paper, there is no reason to restate or recreate the idea. I think it is necessary to have something to say before beginning but too often I see students who will become discouraged because they can't succeed in making exactly what they originally set out to make. They will destroy the endeavor and start again until they finally succeed in producing an absolutely flawless pot which adheres to their original concept. The end result is an academic statement which reflects little emotional investment and loses the art experience. When working for a personal statement, I have found that it is possible to go beyond the original concept by "letting it happen" — by going with the clay. A strange new world of form may open up for one who has experience in controlling these "accidents."

CARL CASSADY

"Bathsheba" by Wayne Taysom
Courtesy of the artist

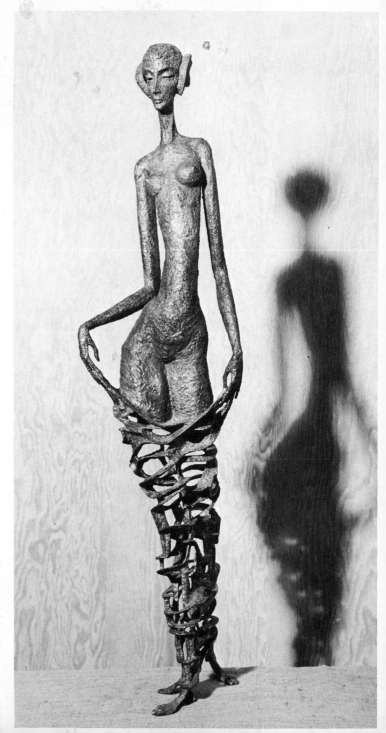

It seems to me that most ideas for the visual arts come from things seen; creatures, objects, movements, light phenomena, etc. These things that one has seen make up one's form vocabulary and are the raw material seen again and transformed by dreams and the "inner eye." By far the greatest variety of forms exists in the world of nature. However, as man becomes more and more surrounded by his own manufactures, this becomes less apparent and accessible and we begin to rely more heavily on things that man has made.

The ideas generated by these things seen must go through some kind of mental and emotional digestive process before they can be used effectively. This process involves our subconscious as surely as sketches and models involve our conscious mind. In addition, whatever we have seen and known of the sculpture, architecture, and painting of our contemporaries and of the past influences not only the way in which we see and interpret things around us but even the things we cannot see and must imagine.

There is another factor which I think is too often underrated. The problems posed by commissioned work many times force one to seek solutions outside comfortable habits of thought and work and lead one to use ideas and forms which otherwise would have been neglected.

Most of my sculpture is built up from steel or bronze rods and sheet with the final modeling being done by welding on additional metal where needed to refine the form and texture. My usual way of beginning is to work from a drawing which is not so much a solution as a note to myself of the basic idea involved. This is redrawn in space with welding rods. It is at this stage that most of the problems that can only be alluded to in a flat drawing become more apparent and susceptible to solving. Next to getting the idea in the first place, this is the most critical phase for one is still creating; bringing something into existence that hopefully did not exist in that form before. The filling out of this three-dimensional outline drawing is largely a workmanlike task, most of the choices having already been made.

WAYNE TAYSOM

Additional Sources for Awareness
and Idea-Exploration

Adam, Marcelle, *Album of Cats*. New York: Arco Publishing Company, Inc., 1964.

Adams, Ansel, *These We Inherit: The Parklands of America*. San Francisco, California: Sierra Club, 1963.

Albert, C., and Seckler, D., *Figure Drawing Comes to Life*, New York: Reinhold, 1957.

Anderson, Donald M., *Elements of Design*. New York: Holt, Rinehart and Winston, 1961.

Argiro, Larry, *Mosaic Art Today*. Scranton: International Textbook Company, 1961.

Aubert, De LaRue, Bourlière, Francois, and Harroy, Jean-Paul, *The Tropics*. New York: Alfred A. Knopf, Inc., 1957.

Baker, Richard St. Barbe, *The Redwoods*. London: George Ronald, 1960.

Baker, Stephen, *Visual Persuasion*. New York: McGraw-Hill Book Company, 1961.

Bandsma, A. T. and Brandt, R. T., *The Amazing World of Insects*. New York: Macmillan, 1963.

Barry, Sir Gerald, et. al., *The Arts: Man's Creative Imagination*. Doubleday Pictorial Library of the Arts. Garden City, New York: Doubleday and Co., Inc., 1965.

Buchsbaum, Ralph and others. *The Lower Animals: Living Invertebrates of the World*. Garden City, New York: Doubleday and Co., Inc., 1960.

Buddenbrock, Wolfgang von, *The Senses*. Ann Arbor: University of Michigan Press, 1958.

Burton, Maurice, *Life Under the Sea*. London: Spring Books, 1961.

Butler, Joseph T., *American Antiques, 1800-1900*. New York: Odyssey Press, 1965.

Caen, Herb, et. al., *Our San Francisco: America's Favorite City*. Garden City, New York: Doubleday and Co., Inc., 1964.

Caidin, Martin, and Yarnell, James, *This Is My Land*. New York: Random House, 1962.

Carrington, Richard, *Elephants*. New York: Basic Books, Inc., 1959.

Clymer, Joseph Floyd, *Treasury of Early American Automobiles, 1877-1925*. New York: McGraw-Hill Book Company, 1950.

Cochran, Doris M., *Living Amphibians of the World*. Garden City, New York: Doubleday and Co., Inc., 1961.

Collingwood, G. H. and Brush, Warren D., *Knowing Your Trees*. Washington, D. C., The American Forestry Association, 1955.

Cruickshank, Allan D. and Helen G., *1001 Questions Answered About Birds*. New York: Dodd, Mead, & Co., 1958.

Edmondson, Charles H., *Seashore Treasures*. Palo Alto, California: Pacific Books, 1949.

Feininger, Andreas, and Lyman, Susan E., *The Face of New York*. New York: Crown Publishers, 1964.

————, *The Anatomy of Nature*. New York: Crown Publishing, 1956.

Fellig, Arthur, *Weegee's Creative Camera*. Garden City: Hanover House, 1959.

Gertsch, Willis J. *American Spiders*. New York: D. Van Nostrand Co., Inc., 1949.

Greulach, Victor A., and Adams, J. Edison, *Plants: An Introduction to Modern Botany*. New York: John Wiley & Sons, Inc., 1962.

Halstead, Bruce W., *Dangerous Marine Animals*. Cambridge, Maryland: Cornell Maritime Press, 1959.

Hausman, Leon A., *Birds of Prey of Northwestern North America*. New Brunswick, N. J.: Rutgers University Press, 1948.

Heinroth, Oskar and Katharina, *The Birds*. Ann Arbor: University of Michigan Press, 1958.

Heller, Jules, *Printmaking Today*. New York: Rinehart and Winston, 1958.

Herald, Earl S., *Living Fishes of the World*. New York: Doubleday and Co., 1961.

Hutchins, Ross E., *This is a Leaf*. New York: Dodd, Mead & Co., 1962.

————, *Wild Ways: A Book of Animal Habits*. Chicago: Rand McNally & Co., 1961.

Huxley, Anthony J., *Exotic Plants of the World*. Garden City, New York: Hanover House, 1957.

Hylander, Clarence J., *The Macmillan Wildflower Book*. New York: The Macmillan Company, 1954.

Jack, Anthony, *Feathered Wings: A Study of the Flight of Birds*. London: Methuen & Co., Ltd., 1953.

Jaeger, Paul, *The Wonderful Life of Flowers*. New York: E. P. Dutton & Co., 1961.

Jirovie, O. Boucek, B. and Fiala, J., *Life Under the Microscope*. London: Spring Books.

Kepes, György (ed.), *Education of Vision*. New York: George Braziller, 1965.

Kepes, György (ed.), *Structure In Art and Science*. New York: George Braziller, 1965.

Kepes, György (ed.), *Language of Vision*. Chicago: Paul Theobald, 1944.

Kleijn, H., *Mushrooms and Other Fungi: Their Form and Colour*. Garden City, New York: Doubleday and Co., 1962.

Klots, Alexander B. and Klots, Elsie B., *Living Insects of the World*. New York: Doubleday and Co., 1959.

————, *The World of Butterflies and Moths*. New York: McGraw-Hill Book Company, 1953.

Kōjiro, Yūichirō, *Forms in Japan*. Honolulu: East-West Center Press, 1965.

Kuh, Katherine, *The Artist's Voice*. New York: Harper & Row, 1962.

Linderman, Earl W. and Herberholz, Donald W., *Developing Artistic and Perceptual Awareness*. Dubuque, Iowa: Wm. C. Brown Company, 1964.

Lord, Francis Alfred, *Civil War Collector's Encyclopedia*. Harrisburg, Pennsylvania: Stackpole Company, 1963.

Manning, Harvey, *The Wild Cascades*. San Francisco, California: The Sierra Club, 1964.

Mattil, Edward L., *Meaning In Crafts*. Englewood Cliffs, New Jersey: Prentice-Hall, 1965, 2nd ed.

Mayer, Ralph, *The Painter's Craft*. New York: D. Van Nostrand Co., Inc., 1948.

————, *The Artist's Handbook of Materials and Techniques*. New York: Viking Press, 1957.

McCurrach, James C., *Palms of the World*. New York: Harper & Brothers, 1960.

McDarrah, Fred, *The Artist's World in Pictures*. New York: E. P. Dutton & Co., Inc., 1961.

Mertens Robert, *The World of Amphibians and Reptiles*. New York: McGraw-Hill Book Company, 1960.

Moholy-Nagy, Laszlo, *Vision in Motion*. Chicago: Paul Theobald & Company, 1947.

Moses, Morris, *Printed Circuits*. New York: Gernsback Library, Inc., 1959.

Muybridge, Eadweard, *Animals in Motion*. New York: Dover Publications, 1957.

Nelsson, Leinart, *Life in the Sea*. New York: Basic Books, Inc., 1964.

Neutra, Richard, *Survival Through Design*. New York: Oxford University Press, 1954.

Newhall, Beaumont, *The History of Photography, 1839 to the Present Day*. Garden City, New York: Museum of Modern Art, 1964.

Nicolaides, Kimon, *The Natural Way to Draw*. Boston: Houghton Mifflin Company, 1941.

Pesson, Paul, *The World of Insects*. New York: McGraw-Hill Book Company, 1959.

Platt, Rutherford, *The Great American Forest*. Engelwood Cliffs, N. J.: Prentice-Hall, Inc., 1965.

Pope, Clifford Hillhouse, *The Giant Snakes*. New York: Alfred A. Knopf, Inc., 1961.

————, *The Reptile World*. New York: Alfred A. Knopf, Inc., 1955.

Rich, Jack C., *The Materials and Methods of Sculpture*. New York: Oxford University Press, 1947.

Rickett. H. W., *The Odyssey Book of American Wildflowers*. New York: Odyssey Press, 1964.

Ross, Edward S., *Insects Close Up*. Berkeley: University of California Press, 1953.

Sachs, Paul J., *Modern Prints and Drawings*. New York: Alfred A. Knopf, Inc., 1954.

Schinneller, James A., *Art: Search and Self-Discovery*. Scranton: International Textbook Co., 1961.

Schmidt, Karl P. and Inger, Robert F., *Living Reptiles of the World*. New York: Hanover House, 1957.

Shahn, Ben, *The Shape of Content*. New York: Harvard Press Books, 1957.

Smith, Alexander H., *The Mushroom Hunter's Field Guide*. Ann Arbor: University of Michigan Press, 1958.

Smith, Maxwell, *World Wide Sea Shells*. Ann Arbor: Edward Brothers, Inc., 1940.

Smythe, R. H., *Animal Visions: What Animals See*. Springfield, Illinois: Charles C. Thomas, 1961.

Stanek, V. J., *Pictorial Encyclopedia of the Animal Kingdom*. New York: Crown Publishers, 1962.

Steichen, Edward, *The Family of Man*. New York: Maco Magazine, Museum of Modern Art Publication, 1955.

Strache, Wolf, *Forms and Patterns in Nature*. New York: Pantheon Books, Inc., 1956.

Taylor, Norman, *The Ageless Relicts: The Story of Sequoia*. New York: St. Martin's Press, 1963.

Teale, Edwin Way, *The Strange Lives of Familiar Insects*. New York: Dodd, Mead & Company, 1962.

————, *A Book About Bees*. Bloomington, Indiana: Indiana University Press, 1959.

Tylinek, Erich and Stepanek, Otakar, *The Animal World*. London: Spring Books, 1964.

Vesey, Norman, *Arms and Armor*. New York: G. P. Putnam's Sons, 1964.

Vogel, Zdenak, *Reptiles and Amphibians*. New York, Viking Press, 1964.

Winebrenner, D. Kenneth, *Jewelry Making As An Art Expression*. Scranton: International Textbook Co., 1953.

Index